DEEP IN THE HEART

DEEP IN THE HEART
The Groom Who Went to War – Aharon Karov

By

RABBI ZEEV KAROV

Translated by
YEHUDA BURDMAN

URIM PUBLICATIONS
Jerusalem • New York

Deep in the Heart:
The Groom Who Went to War – Aharon Kirov

by Rabbi Zeev Karov
Translated by Yehuda Burdman

Copyright © 2014 Zeev Karov

All rights reserved
No part of this book may be used
or reproduced in any manner whatsoever without
written permission from the copyright owner,
except in the case of brief quotations
embodied in reviews and articles.

Typeset by Ariel Walden

Printed in Israel

First Edition

ISBN 978-965-524-175-4

Panim el Panim, www.jewishidentity.info

Urim Publications, P.O. Box 52287, Jerusalem 9152102 Israel
www.UrimPublications.com

Dedication

This book is being published in English with the encouragement and support of Marsha and Michael Lax, and Karen and Yisrael Dov Meyer in honor of Colonel Geva Rapp and the people of the Panim el Panim organization.

We solute their dedication to the educational activities that benefit the Israeli Defense Forces and teachers and youth in Eretz Israel.

Acknowledgements

I am neither a writer nor a poet.
My story is no thriller, and has no plot.
It's just a simple tale about my people.
The connection between this story and reality
Is not coincidental.
Not one detail is invented.
The names are not fictional.
The whole story is true.

Thank you.
Obviously, my first thanks go to the Creator of the Universe, who showed us great miracles with Aharon and gave us the appropriate strengths to deal with the difficulty of the injury and the other hardships.

To my wife Chaya, who knew how to calm, strengthen and to oversee the vast enterprise of our double lives, in the hospitals and in our own home, and whose prayers opened up the gates of heaven.

To my beloved sons and daughters, sons-in-law and my daughter-in-law, who dealt with the challenges together with us and tended to those on the outer circles.

To my mother and to my mother-in-law and to my entire family, who supported, assisted and knew when to be close and when to ponder from afar.

To Tzvia's parents, and to her brothers and sisters, who provided unflagging support to Tzvia and to us.

To the medical teams, to the members of our armed forces, and to the entire Jewish People, who strove to their utmost to help us, and who reminded us that the Jewish People lives and endures.

Thanks to Rabbi Chaim Sabato who prodded and "forced" me to write this book.

Thanks to everyone involved in the book's publication, first and foremost Dov Eichenwald who heads "*Yedi'ot Aharonot*" Publishers, and who oversaw the entire project, and to the book's editor Matat Eshet, who edited with wisdom and sensitivity.

And last but not least, to Aharon and Tzvia, who with enormous valor withstood the great and harsh trial with which they were tested, and from whom I learned a great deal.

Introduction from Colonel (Res.) Geva Rapp

During Operation Cast Lead, which took place Chanukah 2009, I had the privilege of serving as third in command of the IDF Gaza Division. At HQ we heard that "The Groom," Lieutenant Aharon Karov, went directly from his wedding ceremony to the battlefield. Ten days later, we received the initial report that Aharon had been killed by the explosion of a booby-trapped building in Gaza city. Hours later, another report announced that he was in fact alive, but had sustained devastating and life-threatening injuries.

After Aharon's miraculous three-year long recovery, I was filled with joy to participate in his son's Brit Milah (circumcision). Dr. Jackson, Aharon's neurosurgeon, had said soon after the first 18-hour head surgery that "one day you will invite me to circumcise Aharon's son." And so it was! Dr. Jackson was the Mohel for this wonderful Brit Milah.

While helping his wounded son along the long road to recovery, Rabbi Zev Karov, Aharon's father and the head of the Karnei Shomron Yeshiva, experienced a life-changing display of Jewish Unity in the overwhelming outpouring of love and care for Aharon from every sector of Israeli society. What this man of great faith and powerful Torah ideals saw led Rav Karov to seek out and find Panim el Panim, an organization which works in high schools, the army, universities and kibbutzim to help the Jewish People reconnect with their heritage and spiritual roots.

Today, Rav Karov courageously leads B'Yachad, a training program which prepares hundreds of educators who teach Israeli heritage and Jewish values in non-religious high schools all over the country.

Aharon has also recently joined Panim el Panim. The young man who dreamed of climbing the ranks of IDF command, who is also intimately acquainted with the value of Torah and Jewish belief, has become the coordinator of Panim el Panim's flagship programs for the army. Because of his strength, grounding in Judaism and life experiences, Aharon is uniquely qualified to teach soldiers and officers about their Jewish faith.

Am Yisrael Chai!

Geva Rapp
IDF Colonel (res.)
Panim el Panim

Preface

The Notification

January 13, 2009, 7:50 AM, Tuesday morning, the day the Torah twice called "good" (Genesis 1:10,12). Like every other day, I am in yeshiva, at morning prayers, sitting facing north, face-to-face with our students, who are facing south towards Jerusalem. Everyone is silently reciting, "Hear, O Israel! The L-rd is our G-d, the L-rd is One".

Such a Jewish verse, so powerful, so all encompassing! Be aware, Israel, that G-d has not abandoned the world! Whatever happens, it is all from the One, from G-d, Creator of heaven and earth, the Most Lofty and Supreme.

He is also "our G-d", who watches over us, Master of the here and now. Even if the world seems to be moving in contradictory directions, even if we see good and evil, and we ask, "Is anyone in charge?" we must realize that not everything visible on the surface accurately reflects what is really happening beneath the surface.

The "Shema", the Jewish credo, was first recited over three thousand years ago by our Forefather Jacob. It has been recited daily by countless Jews down through the generations, as well as before death. That same declaration was recited, for example, about three thousand years after Jacob, by Major Ro'i Klein, when he jumped on a hand-grenade during the Second Lebanon War to save the lives of his soldiers.

In our yeshiva that same morning, we immediately continue: "Love the L-rd your G-d with all your heart, all your soul and all your might." Total love, which everyone wants so much to achieve and to make the basis of their lives.

Suddenly, out of the corner of my eye, I see two army officers standing at the entrance to our study hall. For a fleeting moment I think they have come, like so often in the past, to announce an army exercise to be carried out in the yeshiva. Another army exercise. Continuing to pray I approach them.

My two feet straddle the edge of the study hall and I see our town security officer, Shmulik. Shmulik is an easy-going fellow with a childlike countenance. Usually all smiles, he now stands behind the officers and he looks different. His face tells all. Scripture teaches, "A man's wisdom lights up his face" (Ecclesiastes 8:1), but Shmulik's face is somber. Lightning-fast one of the officers spits out, "Are you the father of Aharon Karov?" Without waiting for my answer, he goes on, "He is mortally wounded. You must hurry to the hospital," by which he means, "Hurry so you can bid farewell to your son before . . ."

I don't react. I feel as though my body is ebbing out, separating from my soul. I cannot move my limbs. I cannot think, and I feel nothing. How does one walk? Where does one go? What do you do when you hear such tragic news?

Part I | A Bridegroom Setting Out from His Chamber

Three Weeks Previous.

It was the last Sabbath before the wedding of our beloved son, who was serving as an officer in the Paratroopers. On that Sabbath, we remind the groom that he is going to build his home upon a hallowed, vast world of Jewish values, and that precisely those ethereal values will safeguard the couple's simple, concrete bond. The Sabbath, with all it symbolizes for the Jewish People, will provide the philosophical foundation of the bride and groom's private edifice.

That Friday Night is full of singing and dancing, as we bring joy to the prospective groom. Such dancing is characterized by two elements: (1) We lift our feet off the ground, as though to escape the laws of gravity that limit life's potential; (2) We form circles, for a circle has no beginning and no end. It is as though the dancers are forever joined together and interdependent, an allusion to the new, private edifice of the bride and groom – one more circle in the chain of the generations.

And indeed, we were excited and happy over having been privileged to reach this joyful time. We attended morning prayers and the Torah reading. "The synagogue official loudly proclaimed, "Let the bridegroom, Aharon Yehoshua, son of Zeev, rise!" and the congregation sang a tune in his honor. Aharon recited the Torah blessing and chanted a chapter from the Prophets. I, the excited father, heartily thanked G-d for having "granted us life and sustained us and permitted us to reach this season." Parents raise a son, invest in him, experience ups and downs, and this moment fills the heart with great joy — we had succeeded in producing a self-sustaining adult.

All the same, something was slightly souring the joyous atmosphere. At the very end of the service, the whispering began. The Israeli Air Force had just dealt a blow out of the heavens upon Gaza — a small region crowded with people who want to see the State of Israel annihilated. For eight years they had been showering arrows of fire upon the residents of the South, sowing chaos and fear, and filling their lives with loudspeaker announcements about imminent bomb attacks, with ambulance sirens, destruction of homes, fatalities and injuries.

How long would we bury our heads in the sand, complacently leading our own lives? When would we finally take responsibility for all our brethren? These questions troubled Aharon and his friends, and many other Jews. For months Aharon had been preparing his soldiers for Operation Cast Lead. He and his soldiers felt frustrated that they were being prevented from going out on behalf of their brethren, the residents of the south. "War is no picnic," they said, "but you don't abandon your country or your brethren for any price."

After services we returned home for our Sabbath meal. Aharon's MIRS sounded off. From the other end came Ro'i the company commander: "The Air Force is bombing Gaza. Apparently we're going in. Don your uniform and be ready for the call-up."

It came about an hour later. It was Shabbat afternoon in our Sabbath-observant community of Karnei Shomron. No outsider could understand how strange, bizarre and unique was the following scene: an escort of parents, brothers and sisters dancing and singing before an uniformed officer with a yarmulke on his head and a rifle over his shoulder, all headed towards the family car. The officer pressed the car's remote control, turned on the engine and drove away. The entourage continued singing and dancing behind the car for several more minutes.

Aharon stopped along the way and picked up a friend from

Karnei Shomron, a soldier from the Golani Brigade who had likewise been called up to go out on behalf of his brethren from the South.

Over 2000 years ago, the Greeks tried to make the Jewish people assimilate. They killed whoever was unwilling to convert, not because they wished to commit murder, but because they wished to change our religion. Just as today, there were Jewish zealots back then who thought one mustn't fight on the Sabbath. Some said, "We mustn't fight, because every day is a day of rest for G-d." Others said, "We mustn't fight because we do not want war, neither on Shabbat nor weekdays." Both groups preferred to hide in caves and not to come out and fight on Shabbat.

Yet our Sabbath is not divorced from life. Quite the opposite, it enriches life, directing it along the right channels. Not only when life is threatened do we violate the Sabbath, but even when we are uncertain whether it is or not. "Violate one Sabbath so that many Sabbaths may be observed." Gazing towards the future, on behalf of the public at large, is the life-force catalyzing our people. The Maccabees' victory over the Greeks was also the victory of forthright, balanced Jews over extremist Jews from both sides of the spectrum.

Years ago, a friend told me that when he arrived in uniform at the home of his grandfather, a Bnei Brak resident, the man burst out in tears. "Grandpa, why are you crying so much?" asked my friend. The grandfather, a Holocaust survivor, answered tearfully, "I didn't believe I would ever be privileged to see the army of the Jewish People. And certainly I never dreamed that my grandson would be a soldier in that army."

Aharon was driving, despite the Sabbath, as a believing Jew privileged to be an officer in the army of the Jewish people in the Land of Israel.

In the following week, every day rumors flew that the land incursion would take place "tonight". Yet with each dawn it became clear that the ground forces remained grounded. Many Jews were convinced that there would be no ground attack, and the "experts" said the same thing.

Tuesday, two days before the wedding, Aharon's commanders

decided to let him out for his wedding. Two days was the maximum leave he could be granted. Every couple getting married when the groom is a soldier, let alone a combat officer, knows that the groom is building his private edifice amidst a constant need for personal concessions for the sake of the nation and the country. Hence the material preparations for the wedding of a soldier or an officer are generally made by the bride and the parents. The groom is busy in the army. As for his own mental and spiritual preparations, he must find the time to make them himself, and with his intended bride. Aharon and Tzvia, his bride, made those preparations chiefly via cell phone, one of the communications wonders of recent years.

The Voice of the Groom and the Voice of the Bride

It was late Thursday afternoon, a short while before those special, hallowed moments of Aharon and Tzvia and their families. Aharon already knew that some of his good friends wouldn't be dancing with him at his wedding. His best friend, his fellow officers and his own soldiers would not be attending. Many were with their units, waiting for the command, with no leaves being granted. It was not a pleasant feeling, but the situation was understandable.

Ten o'clock that evening, during the dancing, my cell phone rang. On the phone was one of Aharon's soldiers. "Is there any point to our coming at eleven?" He asked. "If we get a ride with the company commander now, will we make it to the wedding?" I felt great happiness. This would be a joyous surprise for Aharon. "Come to the wedding, even later," I answered. I didn't tell Aharon. I thought it should be kept a surprise. It very quickly turn out to have been an auspicious decision not to tell Aharon. A half-hour after the first call, my phone rang again. "We won't be able to come. They've called the company commander for a briefing. It won't end quickly."

Under the chuppa, our tears of joy were tinged with worry. As the father/officiating Rabbi, I recited the blessing to G-d Who "sanctifies His People Israel". And then I added, "Tzvia and

Aharon, reality will not allow you to think the only issue here is building your personal edifice. This is a wedding of the entire Jewish people. Your personal edifice is part of the edifice of the entire Jewish people, part of 'G-d's sanctifying His People Israel.'"

I uttered these words, yet I did not realize that within two weeks this wedding ceremony would literally enter the homes of the entire Jewish people. I did not know that television would bring this wedding into many Jewish hearts in Israel and the Diaspora.

"If I forget you, O Jerusalem, let my right hand be forgotten. Let my tongue cling to my palate if I do not remember you, if I do not elevate Jerusalem over my chiefest joy" (Psalm 137:5), said the groom, together with those in attendance, before breaking the glass.

Jews don't forget for a moment that besides their own marriages, they are bound by other national missions as well. They do not cut themselves off as though the here and now is everything. There is a before and an after, and as a result, there is also a present. The individual is part of the collective, and his life has value only if he lives for the sake of that collective.

The wedding ended, and Aharon and Tzvia droved to their home in Kedumim. Friday at dawn, about four hours after the end of the wedding, the MIRS once more rang loudly. Ro'i the company commander said, "Aharon, you've got to come. We're going in on Saturday night." Aharon called me and asked my opinion. A few questions clarified that Aharon's fear was to be neither here nor there. He would leave his new wife hours after their wedding, but a land operation would not start, as has happened so far.

Aharon called and got advice from Yoav as well, Tzvia's brother. Yoav, a lieutenant colonel in the IDF was seriously wounded in Lebanon. After a long and painful recovery, he succeeded in being rehabilitated and in once more commanding Battalion 13 of the Golani brigade, and today he heads The Tactical Command Institute. In Operation Cast Lead he replaced a wounded Golani battalion commander and he led Battalion 13 in combat.

"If we go in, I've got to be with my soldiers," he said without hesitation. War is teamwork. All the members of the team are synchronized and know each other with their eyes closed. The commander who prepares his soldiers knows the strong points of each, as well as their shortcomings. Over time, a relationship of trust develops between the commander and his soldiers, a trust that cannot be forged with a new commander in a few hours. Soldiers head out to an operation in the name of Israel and for its sake, and there is an obligation for them to go out when they are ready, and when they have the best people and tools. Everything should be the best it can.

Aharon thus set out for his soldiers, whereas the bride and the family remained for the traditional Shabbat celebration following a wedding, short one groom. Doubtless, it was a strange situation. The next morning in the synagogue, everyone was whispering, "The groom left." Many questions arose, involving both Jewish philosophy and Jewish law, about such a Shabbat celebration without a groom. Yet in a compulsory war, everyone goes forth to battle, "even a groom from his chamber". For thousands of years, the Jewish people did not face this question of "a groom going forth from his chamber". For thousands of years, we did not have our own army to defend Israel from its enemies.

Aharon arrived at the soldiers' collection point. The rumors of his arrival passed between the soldiers and the commanders. His soldiers welcomed him by dancing and singing words from the wedding rite: "O give abundant joy to those beloved companions" – beloved companions who were not together for a moment, the way they should be in normal times.

One of the paratrooper officers told me that when Aharon arrived one of the senior officers in the unit cried out joyfully, "Aharon is back!" In other words, not just soldiers need their commander. Commanders, as well, need their soldiers and depend on them.

Going into Gaza

Saturday night, Aharon and Tzvia had a long talk. It was already clear that they would be entering Gaza during the coming hours. Aharon sent an SMS to a friend in yeshiva: "We're going in. We've got to pray and strengthen the Jewish people. The ground operation has begun."

From within Israel and without came warnings against a ground operation. Such an attack would take a heavy toll. "There will be hundreds of dead," said the doomsayers and those of little faith. Every platoon entering battle received several bags into which to place that which no one wanted to place. I recalled the warnings from Operation Defensive Shield. Now, just as then, there were those who tried to frighten others against the struggle. Thank G-d, the reality was entirely different.

Also before blowing up the atomic reactor in Iraq, they were many who warned about how the world would react, arguing that bombing the reactor would not be worth it. There were also those who made a supreme effort to nullify the decision. To their credit, many of them later admitted that they had erred, and that their fears were exaggerated.

The words of Job 3:25 echoed in my ears: "What I feared has overtaken me. What I dreaded has come upon me."

Amit Hizkiya, a friend of Aharon and an officer in the unit, was hit by five bullets aimed at his stomach from a heavy machine gun at a 30 m range. In trials carried out after the operation, all the bullets penetrated the ceramic shield like a knife slicing through melted butter. In real time, however, the bullets did not penetrate Amit's shield. Amit was just thrown aside and buckled over from the blast, suffering a blow to the lungs from the shock waves. "I want to return to battle," Amit told his physicians. When his father was asked about his "militarism" on a Channel 2 morning news program, the father responded, "I won't stop him. Somebody's got to do the work." He was then asked, "What do you mean, 'somebody'? Your son was wounded, and there is good reason for letting others do the work. What about a father's emotions for his son?"

Was that father unaware of the dangers awaiting his son in battle? Yet it would seem that that father knew deep down that his own life and the life of his son have meaning only in the context of sacrificing oneself for the whole nation. Otherwise, why should someone go to war in the first place?

Trembling, I hear G-d's voice calling to Abraham, progenitor of our people, "Take your son, your favored one, Isaac, whom you love . . . and bring him as a burnt offering" (Genesis 22:2), and I shudder at Abraham's silence and at the speed with which he moved on to implementation, without even stopping to shout, "Sir! Yes Sir!" "Abraham rose early in the morning and set out for the place of which G-d had told him" (*ibid.*, v. 3).

Each of us leads a double life. There is our daily life, in which each of us is a normal, average person, smiles and frowns, and has ups and downs. Yet there are times when a person's life becomes a mission. Those close to him may no longer recognize him. They may ask, "Is this the same person? Is this the man we meet everyday? Can it be that he has chosen to make his personal life secondary and to stand fast like cast lead?

As noted, during the weeks before the operation, "experts" warned that the ground offensive would be complicated and would take a heavy toll of our soldiers. "Unpleasant surprises await our soldiers," various headlines declared. Every soldier who participated in the operation was aware of the dangers. Every parent whose son was sent to the front feared greatly for his fate. Amit, Aharon and all their friends knew this. Amit's father knew it as well. Yet it turned out that "Cast Lead" was not just the name of the operation, but a description of the character of those parents, fighters and much of our people.

The operation proceeded on the following dynamic: Soldiers and commanders, residents of the South and most of the public, pressured the government to continue striking at those perpetually seeking to destroy us. The feeling that this was not a local quarrel, but a war against those wishing to annihilate us at any price, restored a cast-lead fortitude to most of the public. It is a fortitude that surfaces only when the nation is certain of the justness of its cause.

Ofer Schpitzer of Nir Banim was interviewed for the television networks. His son, Ben, a Golani Brigade fighter from Battalion 13, was mortally wounded in a tragic error in which an Israeli tank shot at our own forces who were trying to take cover in a building in Gaza. The toll from that tragic incident was three dead and over 20 wounded. Ben was already lying among the dead. In an incident with multiple wounded, not everyone can receive proper treatment. Those providing treatment must decide who has a chance of survival based on what their eyes see, and they must treat those people, and they must leave aside those they think will not survive. As fate would have it, one of the medical staff saw some slight movement, a spark of life from Ben's body. From that moment on he stayed with Ben and began to resuscitate him until the helicopter reached the hospital.

At the time of the interview, Ben's condition was critical, leaving little or no room for hope. He had been lying unconscious for days.

"I have no complaints against the soldiers who fired the cannon shell. This is war, and this sort of thing happens in all wars. Quite the contrary, we embrace you." Thus spoke Ofer, the father, with cast-lead determination. Who was he embracing? Did he know personally the soldiers who had shot at his son? Did he not know that they had mortally wounded him? From whence the strength of a father who sees his son lying in bed like an immovable stone, to speak, and to speak so powerfully? From whence that fortitude?

A few days later I read the words of Amos Netanel, father of Yehonatan, killed in another friendly-fire incident. He called upon the soldiers who fired the errant shell to come to him, because he wanted to hug them. Obviously, he had no complaints, and he even saw an advantage in the fact that it wasn't the enemy that killed his son.

It's hard, very hard, to fathom words like that and strength like that.

It seems our sages were correct in comparing the Jewish people to an olive: the more you grind the olive, the more refined its oil. The public in the South suffered enormous pressure. They were "ground up" for years. Hundreds of thousands of residents, forced to live under a daily threat, under constant destruction, evinced marvelous qualities normally hidden deep away in the collective psyche.

The faith in the justness of our cause, the self-sacrifice, the mutual assistance, the increasing attachment to our heritage – Cast lead all the way!

And I think: "Why only at rare, difficult times like these?" And

I cry out and pray: "Jewish people – show your true self! Why hide yourself "in the cranny of the rocks, hidden by the cliff" (Song of Songs 2:14)?

First Release: A Groom Off to War

Sunday evening, the first day of the ground incursion, my cell phone rang, and I answered. "Hello, this is the newspaper, *Yediot Aharonot*. We heard your son went into battle one day after getting married. We'd like to write an article about that." Sure, it's an interesting story, but an article? "Call this evening," I answered. "A bird in the sky carries the utterance" (Ecclesiastes 10:20). "That little bird has been working very hard," I thought to myself. I conferred with my daughter-in-law Tzvia. Aharon, like many army commanders, is a man of action who avoids publicity. He flees the spotlight, and even eschews group pictures of family and friends, so will he agree to an article?! Yet we know Aharon will do anything he can to strengthen the Jewish People. We therefore decided to answer positively.

Thus, a gargantuan article appeared about an officer who had gone into battle the day after his wedding. All the media outlets – newspapers, television and Internet – were in an uproar. "Was there no uncertainty?" "Shouldn't he have remained with his new wife?" we were asked endlessly. And those with some knowledge of Bible added, "What about the verse, 'He shall be exempt for a year to stay home, to give happiness to the woman he has married' (Deuteronomy 24:5)?" And that's how the Israeli media came to deal with a spiritual issue involving Jewish law: Does a groom after his wedding have to go off to war?

To the outside observer, the secular media deliberating on Scriptural verses and Jewish law might sound preposterous. For days, there were discussions in the media and in the Internet talkbacks. A Knesset member tried to pass a law forbidding the Army from sending a groom into battle after his wedding, with the media attacking him by quoting from the Mishna (*Sota* 8:6): "In a compulsory war, all go out to battle, even a groom from his wedding chamber."

My very dear friend, Rabbi Elisha Vishlitzki, did not come to Aharon's wedding. He sent an SMS informing us that he was with soldiers in the South, and it was hard for him to leave them. He later told me the following story which he also published in a leaflet that came out on the anniversary of the Matriarch Rachel's passing: Thursday night, the day of Aharon's wedding, was, as noted, two days before the IDF's ground incursion into Gaza. He had been asked to strengthen the soldiers' spirits before battle, and to address the paratroopers. At the end of the session, soldiers approached him and said, "You know, our commander is getting married tonight." He answered them, "Mazel tov." They went on, "But you've got to realize something: He's going to come back to us for the battle." Rabbi Vishlitzki was amazed: "He'll come back? To you? And what about the wedding? What about the bride?" And the soldiers answered him, "He's the only one we'll follow into battle. He gives us strength." The Rabbi heard this and he didn't make the connection between the paratrooper officer they were talking about, and Aharon. Only when he finished writing me the SMS, did its register.

In the leaflet he wrote:

"When a groom sets out from his wedding chamber for battle with his bride's support, that is the height of transforming one's private life into a vehicle for bonding oneself to the collective. It is no accident that this incident has become a very meaningful and defining event in the public psyche, and has aroused thousands of honest, forthright reactions."

I am reminded of Gadi Ezra, a Golani Brigade fighter from Battalion 51 killed during Operation Defensive Shield in Jenin, while trying to save a wounded soldier under fire. For that action he was posthumously awarded a citation. That operation was launched in 2002, following numerous terror attacks throughout Israel. Many Jews were killed in Samaria and in numerous cities such as Tel-Aviv, Netanya, Hadera and Afula, and most of all in Jerusalem. The operation surprised many members of our people with its success. Apart from the tragic exception of Jenin, in which many soldiers were killed and wounded, the operation went "smoothly" and struck a mighty blow against the terrorists, a blow that drastically cut down on the terror attacks coming out of Samaria since then.

Gadi Ezra wrote a letter to his girlfriend Galit before the operation:

"If you receive this letter, that means something has happened to me . . .

My beloved, I feel like on the one hand there's nothing in the world I want more than to be with you, love you, build a home and raise a family with you. At the same time, there is nothing I want more than to go out on this operation and to hit those bastards . . . and we have to be ready to pay the price. I am ready to be that price . . . Spread this message, darling: There is no despair – we must always be happy."

What can one say about such words, I ask myself. On the one hand, are we talking here about a mere mortal? How can one knowingly and soberly put aside his personal love and his desire to establish a family with the woman he has chosen? At the same time, is there no truth to the fact that actually, every soldier who goes out to battle is aware that he may not return home? Is there no significance to the fact that every soldier chooses in wartime to push his personal life aside for the good of his people? One for all!

Everyone felt bad for Aharon, but at the same time they were very moved. It was very hard to put on hold the building of one's private edifice which has just begun. Yet the cause for which the groom went out to battle was a great and worthy one, inspiring a feeling of truth and security.

Meanwhile at the Front

From knowledgeable sources we received reports about the special work being performed by Aharon and his soldiers on the outskirts of Gaza. They were the infantryman leading the incursion along their route together with a tank battalion.

Tuesday, January 13. 4:00 AM, a week-and-a-half after Aharon entered Gaza with our ground forces, an operation was planned for Aharon and his soldiers at Al-Tataria. He chose several soldiers for the operation. Additional soldiers wished to participate but Aharon told them, "Don't fear. You'll have your chance."

At one of the houses there, Aharon blew up the courtyard door and after that the front door of the house. He climbed to the second story, in the manner of fighters – with his head up and his rifle barrel ready for any terrorist he might face. Right behind him, back to back, covering from below, was his radio man, carrying dozens of kilograms of gun powder, wicks, fuses and detonators. Two days beforehand Aharon had told him, "Watch out. One match and we'll be blown to smithereens."

Another four steps and an enormous explosion was heard. Later on the radio man, Nehemia, would say he had seen a gigantic fire ball burst forth and rise heavenward from the house. An enormous explosive charge, attached to the ceiling over Aharon's head, had blown up. The entire ceiling disappeared without a trace. The radio man was blown down to the first floor. A large flame filled the stairwell. The radioman got burnt in his face and his arms. The gunpowder on his body mercifully kept its peace did not explode.

Aharon absorbed the charge with his head and his entire left side, and was mortally wounded. The physician on the scene anesthetized him and tried to open an air passage so he could breath, but did not succeed. This involved complex surgery under very difficult conditions. The physician did not give up, and he tried again. He had to find the one and only spot along the trachea that could be cut in order to open an air passage. His second attempt failed as well. "Save him! He's a newlywed!" Aharon's soldiers cried out. The armor battalion paramedic rammed a hose down his wounded, shrapnel-filled mouth, and succeeded in resuscitating Aharon. He continued resuscitating him for forty minutes, no less.

A helicopter from Unit 669 evacuated Aharon to Beilinson Hosptial in Petach Tikva, and the paramedic realized that it was now or never. He looked for the one and only spot through which Aharon would be able to breath, and he cut, and he did it all in almost total darkness. He raised his thumb towards the doctor and the pilot, and he made clear that he has succeeded. "There was an enormous sigh of relief, both for me and for Itai, and it was simply a marvelous, exciting moment," he would later tell the news media.

Itai, the physician from Unit 669, would come to Intensive Care two weeks later, and would cry like a baby on seeing Aharon recovering. "I can't believe my eyes," he would say. And I would tell him, "How fortunate that Aharon was treated by a doctor like you, a human being, a person who weeps over someone he doesn't know."

The medical personnel on the scene and in the helicopter understood that the situation was very grave, but they did not realize just how much. They did not know about the large fragment that had entered Aharon's brain, or about how far in it had gone. They also did not know that hundreds of fragments had penetrated Aharon's body. One time when we came to the brain surgeon, Dr. Jackson, for an examination, he told us that based on the CT photographs, he had thought that at best, Aharon would remain a vegetable. The head of the Corpses Department in the Army Rabbinate recounted that he had been told to prepare for a funeral, "because it would all be over in several hours."

Part II | From Whence Will My Help Come?

The Longest Day

At 7:30 AM officers arrived at our house accompanied by Shmulik, our town's security officer. They knocked on the door. At that moment, atypical for her, my wife, Chaya was deep asleep and another son was dozing in his bed. He heard the knocking and slowly got up. By the time he reached the door, the visitors had left. From the window he managed to catch the officers and Shmulik. Later he would tell me that he immediately understood the meaning of the visit. "I don't know why I decided that Aharon had been moderately wounded, and I waited for their return." Thus, he understood immediately, and decided not to waken my wife. A very important decision indeed. How would she have reacted to such terrible news, I wondered, when I heard my son's story.

Shmulik, the security officer, decided that they would go to the yeshiva to inform me. I was standing at the entranceway to the *Beit Midrash*, the study hall, as the officers informed me, "Aharon has been mortally wounded." My breathing stopped. I tried to collect my body and my ebbing strength and to unite them in me anew. "Mortally wounded?" I said to myself. "That may well be, but there is Someone in control. We know mortally wounded people who have remained very much alive." Was I suppressing

27

bad news? Was I thinking with a clear head, or with the mental intuition that is the result of education?

I recalled my brother-in-law's son, Ariel Yered, mortally wounded by a mortar shell in Gush Katif. The Yered family lived for years in the town of Atzmona in Gush Katif. For several years, they were the almost daily victims of mortar shells and qassam rockets. One shell landed in their front yard when Ariel was playing there. Ariel, one year old, was hit by one fragment that penetrated his brain and another that stopped a hairsbreadth from his spinal column. His chances of surviving, let alone every talking again, were considered nil. I remember my brother-in-law informing me of the injury on his way to Soroka Hospital in Beer Sheva. I set out immediately and I called Rav Firer to ask him to check with the physicians about his status and about what had to be done. Rav Firer called me back after about half-an-hour and told me that according to the physicians, Ariel not come out of surgery alive. From that moment on, the drive was tortuous. I arrived at the hospital about an hour after receiving that terrible news.

I ran to the operating room and precisely at that moment a physician from Ariel's operating team emerged and told me, "You can recite '*HaGomel*' [the blessing recited when one is saved from danger]. Miraculously, he is alive. We don't know what will be with him, but he is alive." Seven years later, Ariel is alive and talks, even though his right hand is very injured and he drags his right foot a little bit.

The Israeli Government abandoned the Gaza Strip, with its astounding beauty and Zionism. And for what? G-d only knows. After all, our leaving Gaza was what led to its rearmament, to the frequent bombings of the south, and, ultimately, to the need for Aharon and his soldiers to enter Gaza.

I also remembered the phone call that awoke us at five in the morning about two years before that, in which we were informed that our son-in-law Yehonatan Lehrer had been very seriously wounded in the Second Lebanon War. I recalled the tense trip to Rambam Hospital in Haifa, during which my brain was in a constant flitter between positive and negative thoughts. Yehonatan, an officer in the Golani Brigade, had led his company along the edge of the Village of Markaba. In battle against Hezbullah terrorists, two of his soldiers were killed, standing to either side of him, a reservist physician who unhesitatingly ran to treat the wounded was killed, and Yehonatan, himself, was very seriously wounded. Thank G-d, Yehonatan recovered from the injury. He was left with damage to his two hands and with a searing pain over the loss of his soldiers.

The officers awakened me from my daydreams to the bitter reality, and they prodded me, "You've got to hurry to the hospital." I made my first decision in life after Aharon's injury: I would tell the whole family that Aharon was seriously injured. Not mortally wounded but seriously injured. "Mortally wounded" sounds like it's all over. The term quickly leads to despair and pessimism.

Our younger son was likewise in the middle of prayers at the yeshiva. He did not notice the tumult outside the study hall. I sent someone to call him out, hugged him and said, "Aharon was seriously injured and we are going to the hospital." We climbed into a cab and drove home to inform my wife and the son who was home. Later that son would tell me that I had never looked so terrible before. It's no wonder.

We returned to the cab and drove to the hospital. When we arrived there, would the worst have happened? Yet . . . surely the universe has Someone in charge. We are His servants and not the other way around. Anything can happen, but I mean anything! The patient at death's door can recover and get better, just as a seemingly light injury can turn out to be tragic.

The trip took forever. During that time, we called the children and the family to inform them. We informed one relative directly and we sent a family member to inform another relative, each in accordance with his nature and strengths. Between one conversation and another, we prayed and pondered, hoped and feared.

By 9:00 AM. we were outside the Beilinson Hospital operating rooms. Nurses and physicians were scurrying around us, not a good sign. They seated us and informed us that the moment the surgeon was able to give us an update, he would do so. In such a helpless situation, there was nothing left to do but pray. "From whence will my help come? My help is from G-d" (Psalm 121:1). The entire family quickly assembled by the hospital operating rooms. Some prayed silently while others wept out loud. Some prayed using their own words and others prayed out of prayer books. Our family and that of Tzvia mingled together and merged through their worries and prayers.

Several days later, it would become clear to us that not just us but the entire Jewish People in Israel and the Diaspora had been praying with us, and still were. About two months after the injury, we were at a wedding. A woman in her forties approached us and told us excitedly: "May I tell you something? At a evening sing-along of three hundred members of secular kibbutzim and moshavim, the singing was halted and they recited a chapter of Psalms for Aharon Karov and all the other soldiers injured in Operation Cast Lead to get well." She added in a confident, determined voice: "We were three hundred secular Leftists praying. For sure he got better through our merit." I thought to myself, "Only among the Jews could there be secularists who stop a sing-along and pray for a soldier they do not know, and they are certain that their prayers will be answered."

About an hour-and-a-half of prayers went by with us not knowing about Aharon's condition. Not knowing is one of the hardest things, for you don't know what you are supposed to be dealing with. Just then the brain surgeon, Dr. Jackson, emerged.

"Aharon is very severely wounded, but his situation is stable at the moment. As long as his situation remains stable, we will continue to operate." He reported to us about wounds to the brain, the head, the eye and the hand. After the fact, we knew that Dr. Jackson was being very gentle with us. Later he would tell us that Aharon was the best example he had had in recent years of the fact that it is forbidden to despair.

Before he left us, he told Tzvia, "G-d willing, I will circumcise your son." Later on he would say that it was hard for him to leave the room without a word of encouragement for Tzvia, and that is what came out of his mouth, yet at that moment, he did not think Aharon would ever awaken from the injury.

About once an hour, another surgeon would emerge, explain

what stage of the operation they were at and what they were doing. They were struggling to save the right arm – Aharon had arrived at the hospital with a tourniquet on his right arm and hundreds of fragments embedded in it. They were trying to save his left eye, which had moved out of its socket . . . Each physician ended by saying, "He is stable so we are continuing surgery."

At 8:30 that evening, fourteen hours had passed since surgery had begun. The doctor came out and said, "We are done. The boy is very strong, so we kept operating for a long time. Now we've got to wait for signs that he is waking up. It could take weeks or more until we see any sign. You need patience." We now know that they didn't expect much, if anything. Deep inside me a struggle was raging. Should I think and hope for the best, or should I prepare myself for the worst news of all? That struggle was decided hands down: to pray and to weep but to hope for the best news possible. What made me decide that? I don't know. A little voice inside me, an impulse, said, "Think good thoughts, even if bad things happen."

Now Aharon was being moved to Intensive Care. He was on the bed – at least that's what they told us. It was impossible to identify him. His head was almost entirely bandaged. From one slit we could see part of his right eye, and that's it. Numerous tubes were attached to his body. From his brain and his lungs, liquids were being drained, there was a respirator attached, and more. It was hard, very hard, to see your son that way, lying immobile and unidentifiable. Aharon, the strong officer with the wide, eternal smile, lying like an unmovable stone.

Months later, when I saw the frightening photographs of Aharon from those first hours after the operation, I pondered the ability of parents to see their son in such a state and not to fall apart. "Shall these bones yet live?" (Ezekiel 37:3) Will it be the same Aharon? These questions would be with us for many days. We accompanied him with a silent prayer: "There is no praise of You among the dead. In Sheol, who can acclaim you?" (Psalm 6:6). And I added a prayer from the High Holy Days, "The soul is Yours; the body is Your handiwork. Have pity on Your labor." The only question left was what to focus on – on Aharon's present appearance or on hopes for a better future? I would look at him and say to myself, "This appearance and this condition are temporary."

The news media came en masse and wanted to talk to us. In the end I agreed to say a few words to all the media together. "We believe in a Creator of the Universe and we believe in Aharon's strength, and with G-d's help he will come out of this," I said. At such times, you don't prepare a text. Nor do you have the time or the inner resources to think about what you're going to say. You say whatever comes out. Your lips emit your personal faith and whatever is flowing within you.

A month later I saw a short film they brought us because at the same time as my interview, in a different corridor, my wife and Tzvia, Aharon's new wife, had said the same things I had said. Neither had been aware of what the other was going to say, and, obviously, the wordings were not synchronized. Was this a coincidence?

"Where do you draw your strength from at a time like this?" they asked me. I don't know. Is "strength" the issue? I asked myself. Such questions and ruminations would fill much of my time spent in the hospital. Later on my son-in-law would tell me that after my optimistic words one of the physicians had told him that my remarks had been divorced from reality, and that it was the children's job to "bring their father down to earth".

An important question in our lives is: Who is the "realist"? Is it the person who contemplates only the here and now, or the one capable of looking into the distance? Is it the one who seeks only to understand reality in accordance with the human intellect, or the one who recognizes a transcendent force?

"From whence will my help come?" I mumbled or said or cried out over and over.

Don't Lose Hope

One of the nights of waiting, I pondered the resources man has for dealing with hardship. I recalled one of the trips to Poland I had made with my students. We were accompanied by a Holocaust witness named Dr. Chaim Basok, who very unfortunately has since passed away. He was a former vice-mayor of Tel-Aviv, an astonishing man blessed with amongst the finest oratorical skills I have ever encountered. Also his personal story, of himself and of his family, was fascinating and unique. He was very elderly, about eighty-years-old, and not in the best of health, but he possessed the vim and vigor of a young boy. We walked and walked a long way, and a student walked alongside him with a folding chair so that he could occasionally sit and rest. His body had aged but his spirit was perhaps at its zenith.

One day we arrived at Majdanek, where his mother and sister had been murdered. Up to that moment, the stories had flowed from his lips with greater or lesser excitement, with precise descriptions of details and insights. Now, we emerged from the gas chambers to the clearing where the beasts of prey had skewered the corpses, and Chaim Besok was silent, and then he began to cry bitterly and to swoon. Those were difficult, traumatic moments for us all. Every single one of us withdrew deep into his own thoughts and pain over the course of all that day.

That evening, our delegation met in the hotel. A student asked Chaim, "How can it be that you still believe in a Creator after what you went through?" Silence enveloped the room, a silence that you could hear in the distance. You could cut the atmosphere of pain with a knife. That silence seemed go on for months, perhaps for years, but it actually lasted only two or three minutes. It seemed like Dr. Basok would not answer that question. He would safeguard the answer within him.

Suddenly, he lifted his voice: "Boys, I cannot lecture you on faith. I can only say that during the Holocaust, my own faith was strengthened." The answer shocked us even more than the audacity of the one who asked it. "How can that be?" I asked. Silence once more. "I saw with my own eyes how G-d took my family to be killed and how He saved me from the inferno. My own salvation was by G-d's hand, no less than the murder of my family. Everything went well for those beasts of prey. Why G-d chose to save precisely me and why the rest of my family was taken, I do not know. I only know that G-d's hand was involved."

Those penetrating words and the thundering silence that followed mingled together, and with that we went to sleep.

The question is, I thought to myself, "Through which prism do we ponder life and everything that happens to us?" I remembered also the story of the wealthy man who set up a shoe factory. He felt he was approaching the end of his time on this earth, so he summoned his two sons and submitted them to a trial. Whoever would withstand the trial would be privileged to take over the factory. "Go to Africa and decide whether or not it pays to set up shoe factories there," the father told his sons. The two set out and traveled around Africa, and after several months returned to their father. One son said, "Father, all the Africans go barefoot. It would be a pity to invest there." The second son answered, "Father, Africa is an astounding gold mine. All the Africans go barefoot, and if we sell just one shoe to every African, we will be rich."

Yes. It all depends on your perspective on life.

In general, I thought to myself, Poland, a cemetery of the Jewish People, could inform us about the Jews' extraordinary vibrancy. How did that nation succeed in recovering so quickly after such a mortal blow? How did it succeed in returning to its land and in establishing a highly developed country that has taken in twelve tribes and more? After going through Hell, how did the Jews find the strength to start new lives and to build families and a country?

I recalled my surprise and wonder at the vitality of those who had suffered the inhuman, humiliating and constantly life-threatening conditions of the concentration camps. From whence the strength to get up in the morning, to perform the horrific tasks imposed upon them, to fight for a crust of bread? From whence the hope that perhaps tomorrow would be better, making it worthwhile to hold on to life by their fingernails?

I received an email from Professor Shalom Rosenberg:

In one of the stanzas of Naftali Imber's poem "*HaTikva*", a stanza we do not sing as part of the Israeli National Anthem, Inber wrote, "Only with the last of the Jews / Only there is the end of our hope!" Indeed, many times the Jews have felt that they were the last Jews and represented "the end of hope". A notable example may be found in the final orations of Eleazar Ben Yair at Masada, according to the description of Josephus (*The Wars of the Jews* VII:8). Ben Yair's words constitute a hymn to liberty:

"Happy are those that fall in battle, for they die fighting for freedom rather than being sold into slavery. . . . Better we should die before becoming slaves to our enemies. Let us remain free men as we leave the Land of the Living."

His was a hymn to liberty, but such liberty was bereft of hope, "for [G-d had] sealed the fate of the Jews." Eleazar Ben Yair added despairingly, "We have given up all our hope." He died a hero's death, yet with the terrible feeling that this was the end of the Jews, that the hopes of the Jewish People were lost. In light of Ben Yair's despair, we understand the greatness of his contemporary, Rabbi Yochanan Ben Zackai, who despite the tragedy, chose hope and carried on the fight for survival. He accomplished this through Yavne and its wise men.

Ben Yair's speech was a tragic example of the loss of hope and the angst of approaching death. Could the *ka-tzetniks*, the inmates tortured at Auschwitz, who barely succeeded in covering their dry bones, have kept up the spark of hope? Was not the death of the Jewish People self-evident? Was hope still possible? Whoever was not on that alien planet, cannot answer this question.

The Jewish partisans were there and they answered, as in the famous Israeli song, "Do not say, 'We've walked our last mile.'" Also those who as they went to their deaths wrote, "Jews! Revenge!" were certain of the future. They refused to accept the pronouncement of their people's death, even though no thinking person could have hoped that the heinous reality would change.

Ezekiel's vision of the dry bones and the "*HaTikva*" Anthem that followed it constitute a demand to make an absurd last stand, to continue to believe in the light, even if the skies are concealed by a cloud cover that darkens the sun. "*HaTikva*" is a final demand of man, a demand to believe that others will be privileged to carry on the work, and that the nation will survive. Yet it also constitutes a demand of every separate individual. Even if a sharp sword is pressed against a person's throat, he is forbidden to despair. He can still fight and win. The prophet concludes with G-d's words, to the nation and to the individual: "I am going to open your graves and lift you out of the graves, O my people, and bring you to the Land of Israel" (Ezekiel 37:12).

I read these words, and within me I hear a new/old melody, with ancient words and a new melody, that has caught on with much of the public this year. Yonatan Razael composed the tune to the famous words: "Not just one rose up to destroy us. Rather, in every generation they rise up to destroy us, and G-d saves us from them." (Pesach Seder)

This song would be sung by Yonatan Razael on Memorial Day Eve, after the speech by Aharon in his first public appearance following his injury.

The "Insanity" Begins: All for One

One of thousands of faxes that arrived at the hospital read:

Aharon!
Dear Aharon and his family,
We wish you a speedy recovery,
In both mind and body.

Dear Tzvia,
We wish you much strength, and that Aharon should recover and that you should merit an everlasting edifice, founded upon joy.

The Entire Jewish People

At 8:30 PM, as noted, Aharon emerged from his operation and was transferred to Intensive Care. From that moment on, the Intensive Care waiting room, hallway and stairwell became like a crowded conference hall. Between the cell phones and the emails from our family members, town and work place, these spots became like an international call center.

Thousands, without exaggeration, came to the hospital, and thousands more sent letters, gifts and everything else. I am not talking about the thousands of our own friends, who certainly came, worried, offered encouragement and assistance. Rather, I am talking about thousands of Jews we don't know and presumably we will never know. The feeling from here, and for months, was that the entire Jewish People was with us.

Two-and-a-half months after Aharon's injury, a relative from Hod HaSharon would send us two new books she had just published. Two books, one copy of each. I opened the books and discovered high quality photographs of newspaper notices, articles and Internet responses to Aharon's story.

One book had about 300 pages, consisting of things written since Aharon's injury until the ceremony in which he was promoted to first lieutenant. The second book, about 100 pages long, covered the three weeks following that ceremony. The books did not include all the articles and responses published, but only a small portion.

There were dozens of articles and thousands of responses. There was a request for people to recite Psalms and requests to know which chapters of Psalms were best to recite. There were blessings, encouragement, thoughts and much more.

"Dear father! I am not a believer, and I am a Leftist in my political leanings. Yet in these times we are one people standing on the watch, guarding one another. Your son deserves the title of a hero of Israel!!! I am proud to serve with him in the same army. I only wish we could know even in peacetime how to live with that same devotion and mutual commitment. Uri, Tel Aviv"

A fax arrived at the hospital: "My name is Asaf. . . . And I wanted to offer you encouragement and to tell you that that despite my being secular, and far from religion, I am proud to belong to the same people as you . . ." The letter continued on and on in this spirit, and ended with a telephone number and an address. I could not resist and I called Asaf to understand better and to introduce myself to the writers.

Or, for example, there was the following Internet response: "Dear brother, I am a resident of Tel Aviv . . . We probably do not agree on this or that political question, but for me that is a minuscule difference. Because in my heart and soul you are my brother. Through your heroism and the heroism of the fighters of Israel, you enable me and those like me to hold the olive branch in one hand, knowing that my second hand is a clenched, iron fist protecting every citizen and child on the streets of Israel."

An elderly Russian immigrant couple arrived with an envelope in their hands: "We took 500 shekels out of our savings for the hero," they said. I tried to explain that there was no need of money, and that their moral support was enough. They did not look like people with a spare penny in their pockets. Yet they insisted, "You don't understand. He will recover and will need money to take a vacation." Not just one immigrant couple arrived and not just two. Some came with 500 shekels, others with 800 shekels. The Russian immigrants believed that Aharon's strength would quickly be restored, and they apparently were very worried about his return to normal life. "Aharon is lying immobile, and they are bringing us vacation money," I thought to myself, and I couldn't fathom it.

A young couple from Kiryat Ono stood before us and wept. They wept and didn't say a word. After a while they quietly whispered, "Thank you very much."

I asked, "You are thanking us? Whatever for?"

And they answered, "Thank you that your son fought on our behalf."

Two adults arrived from Ashdod, shed tears, and kissed out hands and began to leave.

"Wait a moment," I said. "Introduce yourselves. Drink something." "No," they responded. "We came from Ashdod just to kiss your hands."

People came from a kibbutz in the North to offer us encouragement and to leave an invitation to a vacation cottage. They said, "When he gets better he can come and refresh his spirits."

"We are so thankful to you for your having endangered your life for us . . . I am so hopeful that you recover quickly because you deserve to continue leading a happy life." Adi, from the Yonatan Brigade.

A Jew from the United States made a two-day trip to Israel to tell us that he was ready to contribute any sum we might need, and a Christian tourist from South Africa who heard about our case send along a letter and a hundred dollars with a tour guide. Jews from the United States, England and France left telephone numbers and told Aharon and Tzvia unhesitatingly, "When you feel like it, come to us for several weeks. Your flight, accommodations and excursions will be on us."

So they came, day and night, religious and irreligious, young and old, from Israel and abroad, from elementary schools and from nursery schools. They came from the New High School in Tel Aviv, from the Alumot School, from a school in Toronto and from the Jewish Community of France, etc., etc., etc.

We needed a comfortable easy chair for people sleeping in the room by Aharon's bed. I went to a furniture store to look for a suitable chair. "Are you the father of that wounded officer?" the store owner asked, and he didn't wait for my reply. "What do you need?" A narrow easy chair that opens horizontally," I answered.

"You're not leaving here without a chair. Half the price is on us," he added with joy and determination.

"Hello, this is X talking . . . from Eilat," said a woman. If you need a skin graft for Aharon, I am willing to donate it. I feel like I owe it to him." "Who are you?" I asked. "What would make you consider doing such a generous thing for a stranger?" I asked myself, "Is this woman sane?" Several days later the woman arrived at the hospital and talked to us. "For several nights it's been hard for me to close my eyes. Aharon left his wife to defend my country. I feel obligated to donate something important to him," she said. And once more I thought and understood that how a person looks on the outside doesn't say a thing about what is happening deep inside him.

I.D.F. officers with no connection to Aharon arrived and took an interest. The Commanding Officer of the Paratroopers came several times during the first two weeks. He would hug me and then become silent. He would rejoice over every smidgeon of progress. One day I saw his eyes tear. Fortunate the nation that has such officers.

The Hareidim [Ultra-Orthodox], as well, were partners to the "insanity". Thursday Night an older man dressed in Hareidi garb arrived in the Intensive Care waiting room. "Tell me," he asked. "How can I help?" "Do you need money?" I answered no, and I said, "Pray." The same man arrived the next day at 6:00 AM and told me that he hadn't succeeded in sleeping a wink and that he had prayed all night for Aharon's recovery.

One day eight yeshiva students arrived from Yeshivat Ponovezh in Bnei Brak, a yeshiva that is a symbol for the Hareidi public. Their rabbis instruct them not to enlist in the army, but they, too, felt a deep identification and could not carry on their studies as though nothing had happened. They came to express that identification and to link themselves from up close to the story of the "groom who went off to battle from his wedding chamber".

And another day the hospital chaplain appeared and said that the illustrious Rabbi Chaim Kanievsky of Bnei Brak and his wife were waiting for us to come, and they would give us a blessing. The rabbi and his wife are known to the Hareidi public as people who proffer powerful blessings. He took Tzvia and myself in his car. We arrived, and we found dozens of people congregating there, waiting at the front door. On one side, women waited their turns to speak to the rabbi's wife, and men waited on the other side, entering as though on a conveyer belt to receive some advice or a blessing from the rabbi.

We arrived and we heard an announcement in a loud voice: "Everyone leave," and then in a whisper, "The father and bride of that officer have arrived." The rabbi received Tzvia and myself, asked questions and in the end, gave us a blessing. Afterwards we entered his wife's room. She hugged Tzvia and blessed us that Aharon should recover and that they should have children. She also gave Tzvia a book by the rabbi and wrote a dedication to Aharon.

So you see, even the Hareidim, who do not serve in the I.D.F., were excited about the "wounded officer".

So it was without end, for almost a month in Beilinson Hospital.

After a while, the blessings, kisses and thanks spread to the public domain as well: On the street, during shopping, etc., just everywhere. "Are you the father of . . . ? My hat goes off to you! May he have a full recovery," said a young man and woman, and also an old man and woman.

"What is this insanity?" I would ask to myself. "What has happened? Has the country gone nuts? Is this the first wounded soldier in the State of Israel?" It became more and more clear that the entire Jewish People was "not so sane", in a positive sense.

Could it be that a groom's going off to battle reminded everyone that all soldiers conduct themselves according to the principle of "one for all"? Did it arouse in everyone the trait of "all for one"? Did it recall the mutual responsibility and our shared life?

Was the feeling returning that despite all the differences, we still remained brothers? And how long would that feeling last?

G-d Revives the Dead.

Friday, three days after the injury, I called my daughter who was at our home in Karnei Shomron and I asked her to bring me Rabbi Avraham Yitzchak HaKohen Kook's book "*Resh Milin*". Rav Kook was the light source of my spiritual universe. He was a "man of spirit" (Numbers 27:18) in the fullest sense of the term, a genius, and an enormous expert in all realms of the Torah. Most important, he was a lover of his fellow man, a lover of the Land of Israel, and, to my way of thinking, the first man to envision the State of Israel, as well as an architect of its moral infrastructure.

Rav Kook wrote about the new return to Zion, attracted others to the idea and taught about the principles involved. Years before the Holocaust, he wrote about "*Medinat Yisrael*", the "State of Israel" – just so – using that explicit term. Rav Kook helped many people to view all the processes leading to the establishment of the State of Israel as a fulfillment of the vision of the prophets. He also sharpened our understanding that evil and hardship are part of building good on earth. He had sharp and bitter arguments with Ultra-Orthodox rabbis, who argued that one should not be a partner in the nation's return to the Land of Israel as long as that process was being led by secularists. Yet Rav Kook educated towards pondering reality deeply and not being overly impressed by external appearances. I wished to become stronger on that score as I sat by Aharon's bed.

Before Shabbat, my daughter arrived and said, "I've got to talk to you." I saw that she was overwrought. "Something is very strange," she told me. "I retrieved the book and a page fell out of it. I looked and I saw that it was in your handwriting. Did you write that Aharon was ill and was in the hospital? When was this written?" She handed me the page. Indeed, it was my handwriting but it had been written many years before. Like many others, I'd been using the computer for my writing for a long time. I saw that I had written on that page about the harshest trial faced by any person – when one's child gets hurt. Nothing is more important to a person than his children. One's simple desire to live is rooted in the desire to grant life to others. That is how Rav Kook explains the concept of "father".

That first moment, I, too, was surprised and did not understand what the paper was referring to. Yet then I remembered. When Aharon was a year old, he became dehydrated and was hospitalized. There, at his bedside, I wrote the page in question about the difficult confrontation faced by man when his child becomes ill. I had placed that book by Aharon's head, for the great rabbis of Jerusalem had a custom of placing that very book by the head of the infirmed. In the days that followed, I made a unilateral agreement with the Creator of the Universe regarding the relationship between father and son, an agreement that only He and I know about. The *Amida* prayers of *Refa'enu* [for recovery from illness] and *Mechaye HaMetim* [for the revival of the dead] became my most important dialogue with G-d during those days.

For three days Aharon lay immobile. On the outside, he looked like a lifeless block of flesh. Yet under that flesh resonated a life force that was trying to awaken and reveal itself. "Speak to him all the time," said the physicians. "Play music that he likes."

Aharon's sisters and brothers, sister-in-law and brothers-in-law took turns sitting by his side, and they made sure he was never left alone. Our son-in-law Yehonatan was able to draw on enormous resources for providing wisdom and support based on his experience as one who had not only sat by a patient's bed, but had lain in the bed himself, as a casualty of the Second Lebanon War.

Friday morning at 6:30 AM, the Chief Rabbi of the Army, Rabbi Avihai Ronski, arrived. "I would like to go in and see Aharon. I have something to tell him," he said. The rabbi washed his hands with the antiseptic solution at the entrance to Intensive Care, and he slowly entered the room. "Aharon, this is Avi Ronski speaking. Do you hear me?" No response. Did he expect one? "This is Avi Ronski speaking. I wanted to continue our discussion from the day before your going into Gaza." Suddenly, Aharon began to move his hands and legs in every direction, and even his head moved gently right and left.

The nurse who was in the room immediately ran to call the doctor. I ran to the waiting room to call my wife and Tzvia. Aharon hadn't opened his eyes and had not responded to our calls, but he had moved his limbs. The doctors hadn't thought he would ever do that, certainly not just three days after the injury. G-d was reviving the dead.

Shabbat Morning the duty nurse told us excitedly, "I asked Aharon to move his head if he hears me, and he moved his head. I'm telling you, he hears and understands." We immediately ran to the Director of Intensive Care and asked him if he had heard the nurse's words. "When I see it myself, I will know he really does hear and understand," he said, in a tone leaving no room for doubt – the doctor did not believe that Aharon could hear.

Sunday, five days after the injury, the head nurse informed us that the Director of Intensive Care wished to talk to us. "Is it good or bad?" I asked. Fear and hope wrestled in my heart, "I lowered the drug and anesthetic dosage and I asked Aharon to move his head if he hears me, and he did it twice in a row. I am happy to inform you that he hears, understands and fulfills instructions." Our joy knew no bounds. Receiving such regards from Aharon's life forces exalted our spirits. G-d had revived the dead a second time.

One day later, Aharon was already lightly pressing the hands of family members with his own right hand, on request. We didn't know yet whether he could identify us.

The brain surgeon received a report about the situation and

he ran to Aharon's room. He asked Aharon to move his head and Aharon didn't react. He asked him to press his hand, and Aharon didn't react. The doctor said, "They tell me that he responds and fulfills instructions, but only when I see it with my own eyes will I know. For now, I'm cautious."

He still wasn't opening his eyes. He still wasn't doing any more than pressing our hands and lightly moving his head. It still wasn't exactly Aharon. Even so, from here on the biggest optimist was the head of the department: "Aharon will return to himself. Anyone who could wake up four days after an injury like that has special strengths," he pronounced. And I answered/wondered, "It doesn't befit a physician to broadcast such optimism under these circumstances." He answered with a heavy French lilt: "I've got a lot of mileage on me with cases like this."

"Does he identify you?" we were asked, over and over. There wasn't yet any clear answer. There were only intuitions and hopes. Deep inside, we understood that despite the progress, this and other such questions were the main issue. When he woke up, what sort of Aharon would he be?

Tuesday, a week after the injury. We were sitting in the waiting room. Dozens of people were there, standing, sitting, talking or just silent, offering encouragement or praying. Suddenly a cry pierced the air. Perhaps it wasn't a cry but just seemed like it: "He opened an eye and signaled to me with his hand!" his sister shouted excitedly. G-d had revived the dead a third time. During the next four days, Aharon's signs of life would grow stronger and stronger. An open eye, other hand signals and other body movements.

Thursday Night. Suddenly there was a commotion at the entrance to Intensive Care. Benny, twenty-four-years-old, from Kiryat Krinitzi, was being brought in mortally wounded. On his way to reserve duty in the Avnei Chefetz Area of Samaria, an Arab car had smashed into his own vehicle. Benny arrived at the hospital with no harm done to any of his body. He had lost not a drop of blood. Nothing had happened to his nose. His jaw was untouched. There was no damage to his arms or eyes. He was "only" injured in his brain stem.

Hard to fathom. Hard to accept. This did not happen in conventional war, but in the battle against the number one enemy in our country – traffic accidents, a war no one has declared, and to which no one has declared war in response. Yet, it is a fierce, harsh conflict. Since the Jewish State's establishment, many more people have been killed in traffic accidents than in Israel's wars.

About two months later, during the negotiations for forming a coalition, I tried to prod Knesset members to demand the transportation ministry. That is our first and foremost mission. Whoever succeeds in recognizably lessening traffic accidents will win his place both in this world and in the next.

We met with Benny's family. Our emotions mingled with those of Benny's parents, his brother and sister. We are not from the same sector and presumably we did not receive similar educations. Despite that, we had a lot in common. The words poured out about dealing with difficulties and about our personal and national lives, about understanding that life brings a person all sorts of challenges, and about the fact that we do not control our lives despite the fierce desire to think that we are the masters of our fate.

The physicians informed Benny's parents that he had to be removed from life support and allowed to pass away. They wanted to hear it from a second medical authority. Like a vast number of other Jews, religious and irreligious, they, too, sought the advice of Rabbi Firer, who represents a remarkable phenomenon in Israel.

Benny's noble parents made the decision to donate Benny's organs to save lives. The desire to continue living, including the desire to be a partner in the enterprise of granting life to others, coursed through their veins. They chose life, with all the terrible pain they had suffered. Their beloved son had passed away, and so tragically. They could have let their pain suck them into the abyss. Yet they chose life, allowing for a number of varied vehicles of life, all different, to flourish. They could have withdrawn into their private pain and not thought about others whom they do not know, and perhaps would never ever know.

Benny did not merit a "revival of the dead". Why? Only G-d

knows. Yet he was privileged to grant life to others. G-d willing, he will merit life in another world.

Often, in discussions of the great miracle involved in Aharon's recovery, there were some who asked/said: "If so, why was he injured?" Some ask why, while others are preoccupied with the reality and with the challenge that lies ahead. The fact is that Aharon was mortally wounded. The fact is that he was miraculously recovering. We need to deal with these two facts.

Descent for the Sake of Ascent

Sunday afternoon, a week-and-a-half after the injury, Aharon was more somnolent than he has been in recent days. He had also stopped communicating. His temperature was high and he seemed not to be reacting to the antibiotics he was receiving. The doctors were deciding what to do. An expert in infectious diseases was brought in from Afula by cab. It was an unbearable feeling. In a certain sense, it is worse than those first days when he lay there like a lump of flesh. After all, he had already shown signs of life. How could he now be making an "about face"?

Was this a regression from redemption, or a "descent for the sake of ascent"?

The main question was: to operate or to wait? On Monday at 2:00 AM we were summoned to the physician. "We've decided to operate," he said. "We'll open up his head and see what's going on there," he added, as though speaking about a plumbing pipe or a fuse box.

The tension was sky high. Would the operation be beneficial? Would we return to the progress we had enjoyed up until several days ago? In the end it was decided to wait until the morning hours so that the surgeon, Dr. Jackson, who had operated on Aharon and had seen his brain directly, would be the one to operate and would encounter Aharon's brain cells once more.

In the morning, we waited for the end of another patient's operation, and for the operating room to empty out. Sometimes operations take a long time and sometimes they're short. That's how it is. With such operations, it's very rare for the original plan to be fully executed.

At 4:00 PM, an operating room nurse informed us that the operation had begun. "It will be all right," she added. Was that just a nurse's regular mantra or was she perhaps speaking out of faith or prayer?

In the waiting room, a Russian immigrant suddenly turned to me and asked in a heavy accent: "I was told to say the Psalm that begins with the words, '*LaMenatzeach Ya'ancha*.' Could you please tell what that is?" I open up Chapter 20 of Psalms for her: "G-d will help you on your day of suffering . . . He will send His assistance from His holy abode." Amen.

An hour-and-a-half later, the surgeon appeared. He looked tired, but he was smiling. "Thank G-d, everything is all right. The operation was successful," he said.

"What was 'successful' about the operation?" I asked myself. "After all, we don't know what will happen with Aharon. Will he return to his old self a hundred percent, or only fifty percent or twenty-five percent?" But that was not the surgeon's intent. Everyone is an expert in his own, limited field. That's the way the world is. Every professional looks at his job and his profession as though it were the entire universe. What he meant was that the operation, per se, had proceeded successfully. It could definitely be that, as the saying goes, "the operation was a success but the patient is dead", G-d forbid.

Yet the world is more complex and involved than that, as are man's body, his soul, and his recovery from illness.

Once more, from Aharon's brain emerged tubes tube whose task it was to collect the blood accumulating due to the operation. We accompanied Aharon with a silent prayer: "There is no praise of You among the dead. In Sheol, who can acclaim you?" (Psalm 6:6), and we focused on our faith that what seems on the surface like a descent is not necessarily what is happening below the surface, but conceals within it the buds of an ascent.

This faith is deeply rooted within us from time immemorial. During the Six Day War I was an elementary school pupil. Our "bomb shelter" consisted of sandbags piled up to the height of a man at the bottom of our stairwell. As far as the gloomy atmosphere that reigned in Israel I learned about that only years later. The sad joke going around was this: "The last person leaving the country should turn off the lights."

That war took place only nineteen years after the State's founding. Fear gnawed at our hearts: Would the State of Israel be a passing phenomenon, as many people throughout the world hoped and prayed it would be? Broad expanses in all sorts of areas around the country were prepared to receive the casualties. Thousands of graves were dug.

Yet not everything that can be seen on the surface is what is really happening below the surface. Within six days, the Jewish People were victorious and returned to the places where our ancestors lived many hundreds and thousands of years ago.

By contrast, on the eve of the Yom Kippur War, everyone was complacent. A good friend told me that when he received his call-up notice on Yom Kippur, and they knew that the war had broken out, he told his mother, "Don't forget to buy me the four species [required for the *Succot* holiday that comes five days after Yom Kippur. See Leviticus 23:40]. The war will probably be over by then. In the last war, six days sufficed, so now we'll finish it faster." He said these things, but he was not home for *Succot*. He was severely wounded in the war. He came home, but not for *Succot*.

On the third day of the Yom Kippur War, voices of despair were being heard from several I.D.F. commanders in the country's North. The Syrians had stormed the North with hundreds of tanks and they were already on the Golan Heights. The heroism of Avigdor Kahalani, who succeeded in halting and driving out the Syrian tanks, began to restore the color to the cheeks of senior commanders. Amidst the fighting, General Yanush Ben Gal told Avigdor Kahalani over an I.D.F. field radio, "You are a hero of Israel!"

Already at the Exodus from Egypt we learned this important principle of life. Moses met with Pharaoh and said, "Let my people go," and Pharaoh's response was to worsen the Israelites' work conditions. Moses was alarmed and he returned to G-d and complained, "Ever since I came to Pharaoh . . . he has dealt worse with this people" (Exodus 5:23). G-d responded, "You shall soon see what I will do to Pharaoh" (6:1), by which He meant, "You have to learn to look at life differently. You must put on different eyeglasses so that you can see reality correctly. Very often, descent comes for the sake of ascent.

Thus, Wednesday Morning, the second week after the injury, the morning after the second operation, Aharon woke up. He opened up his two eyes all the way. Let me repeat this. They were open wide. Eyes we had not yet seen.

Aharon was lying in Room One in Intensive Care in Beilinson Hospital. On one side of the room was a window that opened out on an external corridor. The window was about five meters away from Aharon's bed. From there, family and friends would peak in at Aharon. When they wished, medical staff or family would close the curtain, and when they wished, they would open it.

Suddenly, Aharon signaled with a hand towards the window. He had identified his brothers and his sister, and he signaled to them to come. They signaled back that they would not come in, because only two were allowed entry to his room at a time. He, in his determined way, signaled to them to come in all the same.

Aharon could now see, identify people, and he knew what he wanted. G-d had revived the dead a fourth time.

It was two-and-a-half weeks after the severe injury. Who would have believed that his condition would already have so improved? Even the greatest optimist, even those with the strongest faith, could never have thought, never have imagined, that Aharon would improve so quickly.

Yet he still had a long way to go. It was very hard to fathom the two sides of the coin. On the one hand, there was Aharon's amazing, miraculous progress. At the same time, there was his present condition, still lacking so much. We could not know how he would look at the end of the process.

Part III | Between Body and Soul

The Media Provides Strength and Draws Strength in Return

From the moment it became known that the paratroops officer mortally wounded was the same one who had gotten married and gone out to war one day later, we had no rest. There were requests for interviews, status reports, etc. There was no media service that did not approach us with a request for a major article before Passover or Israel Independence Day. The wedding was broadcast over and over, and went into many homes in Israel. Aharon's condition and the family's mood were constantly deliberated on.

Journalists sat with us during the wee night hours after sending off their dispatches. They sent flowers, as well as all sorts of letters of encouragement, some quite moving. A writer who had already interviewed us called once more. I asked if she wanted to interview us again. "No," she said, "Save my number, and if you need any help, I'll be happy to provide it." Another interview stopped because the journalist had started crying. He dried his tears and then we continued.

"Aharon's path has given the Jewish People the opportunity to feel national pride once more. Once again the Jewish People are privileged to remember and to feel the profound meaning of being a Zionist, of being part of this nation," wrote a news woman from Channel 10, who asked to meet with Aharon, and explained in a detailed letter why it was important for her to make a film about him.

Or, for example, there was the letter from Channel 2: "What motivates us is a sense of duty to report on something that doesn't always receive the fullest attention in this country, namely, the readiness to sacrifice for the sake of this country and the people who live here, and to guard it in every way. Although the expression 'love of the land' sounds naïve nowadays, right now, during the week before Memorial Day and the Independence Day, I am saying these things in total sincerity." The journalist goes on at length, sharing her feelings in great detail.

One morning I drove to the Channel 2 Studio for an interview.

I was asked, "How do you explain the high rate of participation by soldiers from your sector? Does the great fortitude revealed during the operation stem from your sector's faith?"

And I answered, "I don't think it's just our sector." "Look," I said. "Ben Schpitzer and his father, who are not from our sector, have shown enormous fortitude. Another example: We heard the father of Amit Hizkiya, who was wounded, say that if his son wants to go back into battle he won't stop him. Why do you say it's just the National Religious?" I did not know that I would get seriously dressed down for these words.

I returned to the hospital. Yoske, Ben Schpitzer's grandfather and a marvelous person, greeted me. In our country, people like that are called "the salt of the earth". A man of ideals, a gracious person, and enormously devoted to his beloved grandson. "You really insulted me," he said, in a serious, angry tone. I did not understand what had happened. Surely I hadn't meant to insult a person like Yoske. "What? Are the two of us not from the same sector? We're not one nation? I don't understand you."

I felt a sharp stab in my heart. I was filled with shame. "How did I fall into the 'sector' trap?" I castigated myself. How right Yoske was! Look how they are praying, worrying, offering encouragement and assistance to Aharon.

From Yoske's rebuke I also learned about the caution and precision we must have before we open our mouths. Scripture warned, "Death and life are in the power of the tongue" (Proverbs 18:21).

I am not a big media fan. Quite the opposite. The media, which is accused of being Leftist and far removed from faith, does not rush so quickly to embrace people like me or to give us such a generous chance to express ourselves, nor to stories of faith and Zionism. I think the media very often distances people from one another and fans the flames of hatred. Obviously, one can't generalize, and the media includes different types of people, but my general impression is that they often focus on the half-empty glass.

Yet in Operation Cast Lead in general, and as far as Aharon's specific story, even the media associated themselves with it. The cynics said, "They're doing this to get a good news item." But even if that's true, there's nothing wrong with that if it's done honestly and with integrity.

Still, why did they continue covering our story over all the others? I am not naïve. My professional pursuits require a profound understanding of interpersonal relations. I think I can discern when people are genuinely sensitive, excited or empathetic, even if they are "just" journalists. Telephone calls that show an interest, letters, requests to do interviews or to make films about Aharon and our family – all this and more indicated their attitude. Since the injury, for three months there was not one week without five or six requests for articles, interviews, documentary films or whatever. "Aharon's story arouses a positive approach to Zionism and to self-sacrifice," they said. And they kept on saying it, never letting up for seven months after the injury, and even a year-and-a-half. They never forgot during all that time, continuing to invite Aharon for interviews.

The intensity of the public's response was not clear to me either. The sympathy for a wounded groom was understandable, but it didn't end with that. "You people give us strength. Well done!" I heard that sentence hundreds of times. I didn't understand. What about our reports "provided strength"? In any event, Aharon's motto was "to strengthen the Jewish People", and not just his alone. The feeling was of a partnership with the entire Jewish People. They were all Aharon's parents and brothers.

Just Not the Brain

"I am prepared for him to not have arms. Just let his brain be all right," said the mother of one of the wounded in the Intensive Care Waiting Room at Beilinson. It was the same with us when we were driving to the hospital, not knowing details about Aharon's injury. Each of us said in his heart, "Just not the brain". I would hear that sentence many more times in the hospitals we spent time in with Aharon. "Can he identify you?" we were asked countless times, many more than we were asked if he moves his limbs.

There are times when everyone realizes what is important in life and what is secondary, I thought to myself. In daily life, many people view wealth and external appearances as what counts. True, they will occasionally toss a small bone to the spirit to quiet their consciences, but their main attention will be on the body. And yet, there are times when a person is ready to give up parts of his body and all his wealth, just as long as his spirit will live and remain fully vibrant. "Why does this happen so little in life?" I asked the person sitting beside me. "Why does our feeling of Jewish unity only rarely reveal itself, and then only briefly?" I wondered.

My interlocutor was a friend who was severely wounded in the Yom Kippur War and fell into Egyptian captivity. He was not a combat soldier, but had been sent to an army outpost as a prayer leader and Torah reader. The Egyptian commando attacked his outpost, the famous Hamezah outpost, and he had no idea how to operate the tools of warfare. Even his personal weapon he barely knew how to use. As he fought against the Egyptian commando, he learned how to operate military equipment. He fought with a courage that later earned him an Israeli medal of valor.

During the fighting, he was wounded by an Egyptian shell. Not one part of his body was spared. His eyes couldn't see. One arm hung by a thread, his abdominal cavity was severely wounded and he couldn't walk. Yet my friend decided to live. Towards that end he had to reach the bunker, where our physician could treat him.

He could not see and he could not walk. He decided to shout "The L-rd is G-d" and to lurch his body forward. Yet how did he know where he was? By moving his head back and forth, he tried to understand where he was and in which direction to move. Jump! The L-rd is G-d! Jump! The L-rd is G-d! Finally another soldier saw him and brought him into the bunker. There, he was examined by the famous Dr. Verbin, who wept on seeing his condition.

He went with his severe injuries into Egyptian captivity, where, obviously, he was not treated properly. When he understood that if they didn't amputate his arm he would die of the infection, he "forced" the Egyptian doctor to amputate his arm almost up to the shoulder, thereby saving his life through his own efforts.

Thirty-five years later he shared his thoughts with me: "You realize your body cannot survive in the severe state I was in, and you discover that man has an enormously strong spirit that can keep the body alive and enable it to deal with impossible situations. We are not taught to look at life from that perspective. We are taught to view the body and man's physical and economic prowess as what is important. We live with this superficiality, so we only rarely confront our spiritual world."

The culture we live in endlessly bombards our senses with stimuli aimed at the body. Very few stimuli are directed at our spiritual being. This conflict between the attention demanded of us by our physical side, on the one hand, and by our mind and spirit on the other, the correct balance between them, and the relationship between the two, constitute life's greatest challenge.

"Why is it that precisely as we grow older and our physical side deteriorates, we feel more mature and we want another chance? Is that not proof that Creation is flawed? Our spiritual side matures when we are older, and precisely when we are younger and more vigorous we are psychologically and spiritually less mature."

I am asked this question in a Ra'anana restaurant. I have left the hospital to celebrate the fiftieth birthday of a family member. Perhaps the answer lies within the question. We are more open to spirituality when we are older because our material world is less dominant at those ages.

"The question is," I respond, "What are the goals that a person sets for himself at every stage of his life? Based on that we can examine the question of life and the question of whether or not Creation is flawed. Quite the contrary, we see marvelous intelligence here."

The questioner grew up in the United States. Until his bar mitzvah, he was a child like any other. After that the problems began. His life took many turns until he finally hit rock bottom. He would sleep in the street, endangering his life many times for many years. We have already said that life has its surprises. Last year he ended up in Israel, and now he lives here. That's they way it goes in Israel. Sometimes it spits out its inhabitants and sometimes it attracts people.

"I fell as far as one can fall in this life, but I was always careful about one thing: I always wore *tzitzit* [ritual fringes. See Numbers 15:38] under my shirt. I have no explanation of why I did that. Everyone I hung around with thought I was crazy and they didn't understand. I didn't understand either. But I was always careful about this."

As I have already said, not everything visible on the surface is really what is happening below the surface.

"The State of Israel may not believe in miracles, but it very much takes them into account." This sentence, attributed to Pinchas Sapir, may very well express our entire relationship to our psychological and spiritual forces, and to reality. On a daily basis, we are realists and pragmatists. Yet sometimes we know full well that beyond rationalism and pragmatism lie prodigious psychological and spiritual forces within man and within the world.

Salute

Tuesday, precisely three weeks after the injury, when Aharon was about to move to Rehabilitation at Tel HaShomer Hospital, Dr. Jackson asked to speak with him and his family.

"You must agree to be photographed as you leave, so people will realize they mustn't give up hope. You are the proof to every mother and father fighting for the lives of their loved ones that anything is possible." Aharon nodded his assent.

Three weeks had passed since the injury, three weeks we had

spent in the hospital day and night, Sabbaths and weekdays. Was this a nightmare we would wake up from momentarily? No, this was definitely the reality. At the time, quite a number of people were asking whether or not I question why; and whether I harbor anger. I would try to recall, and to look for moments like that, but I couldn't recall any. Absolutely not. I had been educated to deal with the reality before me, and not to wallow in anger of that sort. Such questions don't bother me. Is that all right? Is there something about me that isn't normal?

For three whole weeks we'd been teetering on the brink between leading private lives and sharing our lives with the public, striving to strike a balance. The entire Jewish People were offering support, encouragement and prayer and were justified in taking an interest out of concern and partnership. We had to be professional jugglers to expose our lives enough for the public to be partners, without their encroaching. The very act of writing this book/diary left me feeling like an acrobat in no small degree. I did not know if my words would ever be publicized, but I wrote as though they would.

We descended in the elevator. Our excitement was great. We had been privileged to see the unbelievable happen. Just three weeks after being mortally wounded, Aharon was moving to Rehabilitation. He was in a wheelchair, still with a feeding tube down his throat. We still had not heard his voice. His eye-contact with us was still not what it had been.

An army of media representatives were on hand. It was as though momentarily the President of the United States, or some other enormously influential figure, would be making a very critical speech. Not one media organization was missing. Aharon was in shock, and so were we.

Professor Singer spoke of the unbelievable pace of Aharon's recuperation. "Karov constantly surprises. This morning he entered our morning staff meeting and thanked the physicians personally for the treatment he received." These words became the headline of the newspaper *Ma'ariv*. Aharon had gone in with people supporting him from both sides and had thanked the staff with hand gestures. He still couldn't talk. The article quoted Professor Singer, director of Intensive Care: "We were pessimistic and we thought his hours were numbered."

Dr. Jackson saluted Aharon, and Aharon returned the salute.

The story of Aharon's leaving Beilinson Hospital, and especially of the salute, drew over a thousand talkbacks in two days – the largest such number on the Internet, as was explained and demonstrated to us by people in the know. We were enormously excited by the quantity of responses, all the more so on reading their content.

"The Jewish People are happy," wrote one. "That's understandable," I said to myself. Such identification with Aharon's story generated happiness when his situation improved.

"Israel lives!" wrote several in response to the article. Yaniv of Ramat Aviv wrote, "How fortunate you are, Jewish People! I've got tears in my eyes."

"Why 'Israel lives' and not 'Aharon lives'?" I wondered.

One who signed herself "Secular" wrote, "I am proud to be part of this nation, proud that I served in this army, and I wish the officer joy and health, and pray for his welfare in my own way."

Avi of Ashkelon wrote, "Aharon Karov, precious individual! Thank you for the privilege of seeing a noble, astonishing act by you and your family. As a reserve soldier in the I.D.F. I am proud to fight by your side for the survival of the State of Israel. Aharon, in my own name, and in the name of every Jew who is proud of his country, thank you, thank you, thank you."

Uri of Petach Tikva wrote, "By the way, your family is all of us."

Yoav Shaul of North America wrote, "Your personal story is our collective story as a nation, which always succeeds in rising out of the dust and the ruins and coming back to life."

In those talkbacks, every one was saluting everyone else, all those wounded in the operation, and all the fighters. "I don't know you but I love you." "I don't know you but I admire you . . ." "I salute you."

In a moving article published in the Internet Site *ynet*, Meir Ben Meir wrote, "Aharon, "while you were sleeping," as the saying goes, since your being wounded in the Gaza operation, great things have happened to your people that you would certainly be proud of . . . And now, Aharon, you will certainly ask and want to know: Is anything left of it all? Is that magnificent spirit that swept us all away continuing to pulse? Hand on my heart, Aharon, I want to believe it is.

Yet I am not always sure. From the window of the car you were traveling in (from Beilinson to Tel HaShomer), you must certainly have passed enormous signs with election propaganda, full of personal insults . . . True, we seem to have reverted to our dull routine, but we still do bear with us that magnificent spirit. Perhaps in a lower dosage, but that spirit still holds strong within us. The best proof that something of all that goodness remains is the very fact that people are taking an interest in you, that they are thinking about you, that they view you as a hero and a figure worthy of emulation, that they speak about you during their lunch breaks from work . . . This little bit is not a little bit at all. It implies a path, a direction, a clear, unequivocal indicator for Israeli society and its leaders regarding values."

I recalled the contradictory expressions used by Haman when speaking to Ahasuerus: "There is one people, scattered and dispersed among the other peoples" (Esther 3:8). If they are "scattered and dispersed," how can they be "one people"? It follows that when necessary, a people that is "one people" knows how to shed all its differences.

Reading Ben Meir's article made me appreciate my people all the more.

The salutes to Aharon continued even outside the world of talkbacks. Two-and-a-half months after the injury, I drove with him to a medical board meeting at Ichilov Hospital in Tel Aviv. When we finished, we were hungry, so I asked him if he wanted to go to a restaurant. We drove to "Entricot" in Petach Tikva. We unobtrusively seated ourselves. A waitress brought us a menu, and after a few minutes she arrived to take our orders. As she was writing, a fellow approached and whispered something in her ear, which only by accident I managed to hear: "Don't open a tab. This will be at my expense." "I saw the surprise on her face and I probably looked the same way. A few questions clarified that the young fellow was one of the establishment's owners, and that he had identified us. Had I not asked him anything, he would not have said a word. He wanted to pay discreetly, "as a mark of thanks to Aharon for his heroism".

Aharon and I were in the car, on the way to yet another medical expert. At a traffic light, the driver to our right signaled that we should open the window, as though wishing to ask directions. I opened the window and the driver began to shout, "I salute you, heroes!" Aharon seemed embarrassed, and he asked me how the man had identified us. "Wait, do they identify you or me?" Aharon asked, and then quickly, "They identify you," to which I replied, "No, they identify you."

For a while I've been thinking that all the bestowers of blessings and salutes are simply identifying themselves, their true face under all the masks.

The Beginnings of Speech

At Tel HaShomer they began a thorough examination of what damage Aharon had suffered due to his brain injury. Besides all the physical tests, they also tested his memory. Did he understand? Did he remember? And if so, how much?

Aharon couldn't talk yet, and the test was carried out via writing questions on a blackboard and writing four answers for each one. Aharon was supposed to point at what he considered the right answer. "Who was the rabbi who officiated at your wedding?" Slowly we drew nearer to the questions tied to the fighting in Gaza. "Who was your first soldier who got wounded?" Aharon pointed at the right name! I ventured to ask, "Which part of his body was hurt?" Without hesitation, Aharon indicated the palm and the hip.

It turned out that Aharon remembered nearly everything, except for what happened starting from an hour before the beginning of the incursion until his transfer to Tel HaShomer. Sometimes he got confused and did not know if he was in Beilinson or Tel HaShomer. It really hurts to see your son in that condition. Fears of what shape he will be in in the future can really shake you up. Yet the more time passed, the more Aharon became synchronized with reality.

A month-and-a-half after the injury, a speech therapist at Tel HaShomer was trying to help Aharon begin to talk. She closed the opening in Aharon's throat. It seemed as though Aharon Karov was nowhere near being able to speak. He did not succeed in uttering even one sound.

Deep down I was disappointed. Once more I was faced with the question of what sort of eyeglasses I was wearing that day, glasses that focus on what has been achieved, glasses full of optimism about a rosier future, or glasses that focus on what is lacking in the here and now.

The speech therapist did not give up. She kept trying every day. Four days later Aharon succeeded in making his first sounds. The difficulty made Aharon revert to silence, and by the time I was privileged to hear his first words, another day had passed. "Dad, everything's all right." That's what he said to me, and I recited the *Shehechiyanu* blessing, thanking G-d for having "granted us life and sustained us and permitted us to reach this season." Aharon gave me a puzzled look, and I explained, "Man is called *homo loquens*, "the speaker". Speech is what distinguishes him. We take speech so much for granted that we pay no attention to this marvelous, unique ability."

As far as I am concerned, that was "Revival of the Dead" number five.

Even after the many miracles we had been privileged to see regarding Aharon, there were physicians who were pessimistic about his regaining speech. The splinters that had penetrated his brain had entered the area responsible for speech, and had done great damage. Aharon slowly resumed speech, and his speech got better and better, but it had not yet returned fully. It also turned out that sometimes Aharon had a hard time retrieving the word he wanted to use.

An ophthalmologist who arrived to examine Aharon's vision asked him, "What number do you see?" and he responded "five".

"Now," the doctor continued, "What number do you see?" "Five", answered Aharon.

"And now," he went on, "What number do you see?" and again Aharon answered five. At first we were alarmed at the possibility that Aharon could not see or could not understand. Yet then one of the physicians asked Aharon to signal with his hand what number he saw. Aharon kept on saying the number five, but with his hand he signaled the right number. We began to understand that his difficulty was in retrieving the right word.

We dealt with his speech difficulties for a long time, and during that period, his progress was slow, but unceasing.

When Aharon set out for Rehabilitation at Tel HaShomer Hospital, everyone could only see that he was missing the left side of his skull-bone, and they were alarmed by that. From all the damage he had suffered, one's eyes headed straight for the recess in his head, and that was more frightening than anything else. People were afraid of that recess, and they were afraid to ask about it, as though it were something frightening and mysterious better not talked about.

Yet what looks frightening on the surface is not necessarily where the problem lies. That's how medicine works. With brain wounds, they remove part of the skull to make room for the brain to swell. As is well-known, wounds cause swelling. If the brain swells and the skull subsequently presses on it, that is not good. Hence they free up a place for the brain to swell until it recedes and returns to normal size.

Two-and-a-half months after the injury, the bone was put back in place. It was one of the miracles of medicine. They sawed the bone, preserved it in cold storage, and then restored it to its place, as if it were a Lego piece.

Early one morning, a week after Aharon's first words, and a month and three weeks after the injury, we were driving to the graduation ceremony of Aharon's soldiers at Beit Lid. It was the first time Aharon was leaving the hospital. He was still very weak and only a short time before had begun to walk without any assistance, and an even shorter time before had opened his mouth. We knew that at this ceremony Aharon would be promoted to first lieutenant. We did not know what to expect. What would Aharon do and how would he behave? How would he deal with it?

Aharon asked his wife to bring him a uniform, and we found one, attaching a set of second lieutenant's bars. Aharon then asked for army boots. I tried to explain to him that he didn't have to wear them, but he dismissed my words with a wave of the hand.

Arriving at the Paratroopers Base in Beit Lid, we parked near the parade grounds. Aharon didn't get out of the car. He found the throngs outside daunting, and gathered strength for the coming ceremony. As noted, this was the first time he was leaving the hospital for the "real world". Suddenly he saw his platoon standing in a "C" shape and the platoon commander who had replaced him talking to the soldiers. Without any warning, Aharon got out of the car, approached the group and signaled to the platoon commander to come over to him. I don't know what he said to him, but with a few words he succeeded in making clear that he wished to address his soldiers. Following the short talk between them, the platoon commander left the place and Aharon drew near to his soldiers. He signaled to them to come closer. I got out of the car and ran to stand behind him in order to see and to hear. Aharon began speaking:

"I would like to thank you for your conduct during the war, each and every one of you, wherever you were positioned. As far as those who were with the folding horse [by which he meant "the holding force"], and those who were with me, I am certain that everyone did . . ." Here he got stuck. I, understanding what he wanted to say, whispered to him, "what needed doing," and Aharon said, "Right, he did what needed doing." I cried inside me, tears of joy. Aharon was back to talking without any planning or preparation.

From then on, the entire ceremony continued almost naturally. Aharon acted as the platoon's commander. He entered the parade grounds together with all the officers, awarded his soldiers their warrior pins and awarded his own pin to his radio man as a mark of his admiration. Aharon was called up to receive first lieutenant's bars. The audience stood on its feet and began a thunderous roar. The atmosphere was so thick you could cut it with a knife. You could see and feel the identification, the sense of togetherness.

"Our most severely wounded soldier from Cast Lead is First

Lieutenant Aharon Karov, who is with us here. Aharon, it is hard to believe that less than two months after your very severe injury, you are with us here," said the Brigade Commander, Hertzy Levi, with great excitement. Indeed, it was hard to believe. Did Aharon and his family understand what a great miracle had transpired? Did the object of the miracle recognize the miracle?

Unfortunately, such is the way of the world. A person or a nation are immersed in daily life and in their own hardships, and they have a hard time seeing the miracles occurring to them. I pray that I will never be like that. I pray that I will always have the strength to ponder G-d's mercies.

The words of King David played on my lips: "Who is wise? Let him observe these things. Let them consider the L-rd's mercies" (Psalm 107:43).

The next day's newspaper headlines proclaimed: "Not an eye was dry on Friday Afternoon when Aharon Karov walked on to the parade grounds . . . Even the Paratrooper Brigade Commander had a hard time hiding his excitement." Aharon saluted Brigade Commander Herzl Levi, known as "Herzi". The Brigade Commander saluted him back, in a gesture expressing total respect and admiration.

"Herzi", who manages to combine practicality, determination and sensitivity, spoke at the ceremony about the weekly Torah portion, and about valor. When he mentioned Aharon, his voice trembled. The Brigade Commander was a man responsible for thousands of soldiers. Yet since Aharon's injury, you couldn't tell that. He visited Aharon many times, took an interest, would grow emotional and would salute. Fortunate the nation whose senior commanders are like that!

I recalled a telephone conversation I had several days after the injury: "Hello, this is Gabi Ashkenazi speaking. I wanted to apologize for not yet having come to visit." The speaker was none other than the head of Israel's Armed Forces. The man's wife had already visited us in the hospital, but he hadn't yet. He felt the need to apologize to the family of a young officer, a second lieutenant, for not having come to visit in the middle of a war. Two days after the operation's conclusion, he came for a visit.

Throughout the entire ceremony, which lasted about an hour-and-a-half, our family was worried and tense. Aharon was standing in the sun, which was particularly hot that Friday. All our nervously gesticulating to him to drink water or to sit down and rest made no impression on him. The only difference you could see between Aharon and the rest of the officers was the sunglasses Aharon was wearing. One of his eyes had been struck by shrapnel and was sensitive to the sun.

I recalled a saying from the army: "There's no such thing as 'I can't'. There is only, 'I don't want to.'" A bit of an exaggeration, but it contains a lot of truth.

To Be a Free Man

It was Sunday, three months after the injury, during the intermediate days of Passover. I arrived at the Channel Two News Station to transmit a morning lecture, live, on the topic of, "Being a Free Man". Before the lecture and afterwards, station workers came up and asked me how Aharon was doing. Some of them asked if they could interview him.

I divided the lecture into two parts: In the first part I clarified what is the essence of man – intellect, will or deeds. We understand that the essence of man is his will. A man can think and know things, but those things are not him. He can know the importance of helping out his fellow man, but he may still lead the life of an enormous egotist. Likewise, he can do deeds that do not express his personality, but are only meant for show. For example, a person can donate money, but that will not tell us anything about the goodness of his heart. The main force that expresses the person is his will. A person can be forced to learn and to know. He can be forced to do this or that action. Yet he cannot be forced to want something.

In the second part of the lecture we learned that the essence of freedom is wanting what we truly desire, and not the desires of others that have been imposed on us.

Throughout Aharon's return to us, what most excited me were those moments when Aharon went back to being himself. I am talking about when he went back to wanting those things that we recognized as his desires before the injury: the desire to eat the foods that he loved, the desire to leave the hospital, the desire to drive.

Two revelations of his will gladdened me more than any other. One was this: Before Pesach, there began to be talk of Aharon's being released to daily out-patient treatment. Aharon said he wanted to set up a Torah-learning partnership in yeshiva. "I want to start yeshiva learning again," he said. "Every day when I finish treatment, I'll go to yeshiva and I will start to learn a bit."

He was good to his word. He made contact with his learning partner from before his officers' course and examined the possibility of their learning together. Yeshiva learning is chiefly built on learning partnerships. Students sit in pairs and learn with each other, explains things to each other, ask each other questions, and, together, "break their heads" to understand the topics being studied. Despite his difficulties with concentration and speech, Aharon overcame his physical limitations and soared in the expanses of the free will.

The second time Aharon revealed his wishes was on Friday in the middle of Pesach. He said he wanted to take a hike. Pesach, after all, falls out in the Spring. We decided to go down to Kana Brook that runs past the foot of our town, so we could return the moment Aharon started having trouble walking. Kana Brook is one of the most beautiful streams in Samaria. It constitutes the border between the Tribal portions of Mannasah and Ephraim. Today, on one side lies the town of Yakir. Scripture states, "Truly, Ephraim is a dear [yakir] son to me" (Jeremiah 31:19), and Yakir lies on the border of the tribe of Ephraim. On the other side of the brook are the towns of Karnei Shomron and Ma'alei Shomron. The flowers are in bloom, and small pools of water are still holding up, inviting one in for a dip.

We descended to the wadi and decided to hike westward along the brook. Towards the east we could see dozens of hikers, and we wanted to be alone. Every fifteen minutes I asked Aharon if he wanted to rest. "What's wrong, Dad?" he asked with surprise and irritation. "Nothing's wrong. You weren't injured and everything is normal," I answered, cynically and defensively. Aharon walked along the wadi, occasionally picking up a niece or nephew. Slowly, Aharon was freeing himself from being dependent on others. He wanted to be independent, and he felt independent, even if there were a small number of encumbrances.

One of the other hikers identified Aharon. I saw his eyes popping out of his head, as if to say, "Hey! You've been fooling everyone. You're not injured at all!" As I already said, Not everything we see on the surface is what is happening beneath the surface. Truth be told, we, too, sometimes found ourselves confused.

"Think positively and everything will be all right." Those words, from Rabbi Nachman of Breslov and turned into a popular song, were running through my head. Much of a person's freedom depends on his attitude to life. When Israel left Egypt, they still thought like Egyptian slaves. Thus when they saw the Egyptians pursuing them, they almost broke down and wanted to return to Egypt. Six hundred Egyptian charioteers were chasing six hundred thousand men aged twenty to fifty, plus thousands more aged seventeen to twenty. About a million of our brethren were alarmed by six hundred charioteers? They still thought like slaves. Aharon thought like a free man.

"Aharon sat down by himself," and there were cheers. "Aharon smiled," his mother tearfully announced. "Aharon is walking," the physical therapist excitedly told the head of the department. How many times during the past three months had we gone wild over things that seem so simple: sight, hearing, eating and walking. The nature of life makes us take for granted all the good things we've got. Our lives *have* to be good. If we can see, hear and walk, well, that's how it's supposed to be. So what does that leave us to focus on? On problems, on the empty half cup.

There's a story told by Rabbi Shlomo Carlebach, known as "the dancing, story-telling rabbi". He was a lover of Israel who strove to his utmost, in his own way, to reach out to everyone and to bring joy to all. The story is about the Riminov Rebbe. When the Rebbe was ten years old, chassidim passed his home and saw him dancing wildly and shouting, "Thank you, Master of the Universe!" The chassidim stopped and asked the boy, "Why are you dancing and singing like that? and the boy responded, "Because I haven't had anything to eat for three days." Puzzled, they asked, "Is that a reason to dance?"

The boy told them that his parents were very poor and they worked hard to bring food into their home. Sometimes they were more successful, and sometimes less, but they always succeeded in finding something to stave off his hunger. Yet in the last several days they hadn't succeeded in bringing home anything.

"I began to get angry at the Master-of-the-Universe and I yelled at Him. 'Why are You doing this to me? What has a little boy like me done to You?' and in the middle of my yelling, I began asking myself, 'During the past ten years that you did have food, did you say thank you to G-d? Only now you remember to turn to Him?' And I said to myself, 'First I should thank G-d for the ten years of food, and then I can go back to yelling at Him.' So here I am, dancing and thanking G-d for the ten years in which I had food."

The Unity of Israel

It was three-and-a-half months after the injury, the day before Memorial Day. That morning we drove to our fourth medical board meeting. Aharon's injuries were multi-systemic, and to determine his disability level, he had to undergo seven medical boards. We were in the clinic of a mouth-and-jaw expert, waiting in the hallway and talking. A girl about twenty-years old came in wearing jeans with long, flowing hair. Presumably she had come to the doctor. She seated herself and scrunched up her eyes, wanting to say something but restraining herself. Yet she couldn't hold out forever: "You've got nothing to worry about. Another year-and-a-half and you'll be as strong as an ox. Take it from me! Eighteen months starting from the injury you'll be your old self," she ruled.

Who'd she think she was? A kabbalistic *rebbetzin*? What was going on here? Were we in the doctor's waiting room or the vestibule to the World-to-Come?

Thinking back on that girl, I have often wondered whether she was offering a blessing or a curse. We had been hoping for and talking about a year to recuperate, and she decides on a year-and-a-half?

Once Aharon began talking again, there were unending requests. Everyone wanted to interview him, to hear him, and they sought his participation in all sorts of events. He continued vociferously to refuse, but he agreed to attend and address the Memorial Day Ceremony at Jerusalem's International Conference Center. "I cannot possibly turn down a request to honor the fallen," he said. We spoke together about what he should talk about at the ceremony, and we raised several possibilities.

Aharon chose to address Jewish unity at the ceremony. In his speech he said:

"In the army I fought alongside religious and secular soldiers, rightists and leftists, city boys and kibbutz natives. After my injury, all parts of the nation prayed for my recovery. Likewise, those who died were killed and murdered without regard for their opinions or party affiliation . . . On this day, we must strengthen the unity between us, focus on our common ground, and less on what divides us . . ."

We take for granted the good things we've got, and we almost always focus on the empty half of the glass. When Independence Day arrives, this is all the more noticeable. The good things, the things that unite us, are taken for granted, whereas we complain and focus on what we lack.

After two thousand years of exile, we are experienced the In-gathering. Every year, more and more Jews live in this country. In such a short time, we have established a country that is strong in many ways. True, there are problems and some things go awry, but how can we fail to be overwhelmed by the enormous good that exists in this country, all the more so considering that all this is happening just years after the dreadful Holocaust, in which millions of our people were murdered and millions more were left broken and shattered, bereft of their families and communities. Whenever President Shimon Peres speaks about the establishment of our state, he stresses that it constitutes one of the greatest miracles of world history.

That Independence Day, I read an interview with Shlomo

Shamir, the last living I.D.F. general from 1948. At the end he was asked, "Is the State of Israel presently celebrating sixty-one years the one you struggled to establish and the one you hoped for?"

"Yes it is, and with several exclamation points," he answered. At least ninety-five percent of our society consists of upright people, who don't lie or cheat, who are ready to give their lives for this country. All the negatives pale in comparison to Israel's strong points." Apparently, it's a matter of your perspective.

At the opening ceremony of Independence Day at Mount Herzl, Knesset Speaker Reuven Rivlin, a Jew in every ounce of his being, mentioned Aharon in his talk. One of Aharon's sisters who heard him called to tell us. She was surprised and we were surprised. We had begun to get used to articles and news reports about Aharon, but that they should talk about him this way at a ceremony addressing the entire nation? That was really surprising. Here is what he said:

"We are used to talking about the heroes of 1948, but there are also the heroes of 2009. We stand in amazement before the heroes of Operation Cast Lead, like Lieutenant Aharon Karov, who sprang forth like a lion from his wedding night to lead his troops into a battle in which he was severely wounded," he said, and the crowds cheered.

And I thought to myself: Once more, bridegrooms are heading off to war from their weddings. Once more, we are yearning for a life in which the public is at center and not one's personal life. Once more, we wish to feel we are part of something great and lofty. Is what we are experiencing a parenthesis within real life, or could it be, perhaps, that what seems like real life is the parenthesis within the reality of the life of our people Israel?

Bird's Eye View

Almost four months after the injury, our family was slowly resuming normal life. On a Thursday we traveled down to Eilat to spent Shabbat with our daughter. The plane took off and we could see our country from a bird's eye view. Israel is beautiful and impressive, with green fields, multi-story buildings and red-roofed houses, Jerusalem and the Dead Sea, the Samarian Hills and the Judean Hills. All are breathtakingly beautiful.

From above, you don't hear arguments between political parties and you don't see traffic accidents. I thought to myself, "What is the true reality? Life as seen from above or life as lived below? The general view or the descent into details?

We landed. Most of the passengers started getting up while the plane was slowly rolling along the landing pad. One of the people who stood up said out loud, "That's how we Israelis are. We stand up even when we know there's still time. We're always in a rush."

The man sitting in the row in front of me asked the speaker in a deep, self-assured tone, "How many times have you flown with foreign airlines?" He didn't wait for an answer and he continued, "I fly a lot and I see this on all the flights. We Israelis are just too hard on ourselves." The speaker stood there embarrassed and said, "You're right, but we've still got room for improvement," and the man in front responded, "We look at ourselves negatively," but then he added, "You're right. There's room for improvement as well."

One day my cell phone rang.

"Hello, this is X calling from Yokniam. Our grandson lives in Boston with our daughter, and is about to celebrate his sixth birthday. He decided to forego birthday presents and he asked to give all the money he receives to Aharon. He told his friends this, and they decided to add money for Aharon and for Ben Schpitzer who were wounded in Cast Lead. The family wants to come to Tel HaShomer Hospital and to bring an album of best wishes and a check for Aharon and for Ben Schpitzer."

What could we possible say to that?

The Rabbis said, "Every Jew is responsible for every other Jew," and, "All Jews are one another's friends." A six year old child in Boston remembered the wounded, felt a partnership and connection to them, and was giving up his birthday presents for them. More than that, he was devoting his free time to collecting money for them.

On Tuesday, the grandmother and grandfather arrived from Yokniam, accompanied by their daughter, an officer in the Air

Force. It turned out that the grandfather, Yochai Yitzhari, was a survivor of the famous destroyer, "Brothers of Eilat". That destroyer guarded Israel's coast from 1956 until 1967. During the Six Day War, the destroyer sank two Egyptian torpedo ships, but during Succot, at night, just two months later, four Egyptian missiles hit the destroyer. Forty-seven fighters were killed and about ninety were wounded. Yochai was wounded by the second missile, but he managed to recite the "Shema" and to jump into the Red Sea.

"I swam in the water for several hours. In the meantime, helicopters arrived and dropped down lifeboats. Such boats are meant to hold five people. The one near me took in about fifty wounded, with more people holding on from the sides. I was afraid that if I held on too it would cause it to sink. I passed up the chance and continued swimming. Only at 2:45 AM was I identified. They pulled me into a helicopter in critical condition . . . Several years later I was wounded again in the course of my army service. That time as well, thank G-d, I was saved." That's the story he told the newspaper years ago.

Yochai Yitzhari, who came to Israel from Yemen in Operation Magic Carpet at age five, remembers well the donkey caravan that carried his family and their meager belongings to the city of Aden. There, they boarded a flight for Israel. They arrived during a harsh winter and had to cope with living in a tent, shared with another family, in the Rosh HaAyin Transit Camp. Yochai, who absorbed his devotion to Eretz Yisrael from his parents, who in turn were carrying on this tradition from their own predecessors, was privileged to see his six year old grandson understand that he must forego his own personal needs for the sake of other members of his people.

I recalled a story that had appeared in the Newspaper *Maariv* about thirty-five years ago. Its title was "Sweety? Got a cigarette?" The story was about a street gang that "took over" a Tel Aviv neighborhood and harassed passersby, or, more precisely, female passersby. They would ask each one, "Sweety, got a cigarette?" and they would harass her. Neighborhood residents asked the police to rid the neighborhood of those boys.

One day, when they were still sitting on the corner railing, a little girl crossed the street. One of the boys saw that an approaching car was going to run her over. Without hesitation, he jumped into the street and pushed the child out of harm's way. He was lightly wounded, but he saved the girl. The neighborhood's residents were confused and they asked themselves, "Who are these boys? Are they the ones that are tormenting us daily, or are they the ones that are jumping in front of cars to save little girls?" Is the reality as it appears from above, when you take a look at the really important things when the going gets rough, or are they as they appear up close when you deal with the small details that encumber daily life?

Yaron Dekel did a radio interview with Gil Schweid, CEO and founder of "Checkpoint", one of the wealthiest men in Israel and one of its most successful Hi-tech executives. The interview was quite instructive. Throughout the interview, Dekel was trying to extract one negative or critical word out of the interviewee, but Gil stuck to the positive and couldn't be flustered.

"What do you say about the phenomenon of the brain drain to the Diaspora?" he was asked. His response was quick and sharp: "I think more brains are arriving in Israel than leaving it. It's very good to live in Israel, better than in the Silicon Valley. I see my Checkpoint workers and I know more who have returned from the U.S. to Israel than who have left Israel for the U.S."

"The government needn't protect the very rich to ensure that they remain rich." This he said in response to a question about the economic crisis. "Perhaps the government has to defend strategic assets, enormous companies so they do not collapse, but not necessarily specific individuals to preserve their wealth." He added, "Now is the time to hurt people like me economically, and not the poor."

"Do you think the education system has failed?" Yaron Dekel asked, and Schweid continued in his positive vein: "I think the education system is all right. I've got a project with youth from the periphery at Tel Aviv University, and they're really doing great."

Dekel's last question was: "It's no secret that you are amongst the wealthiest men in the country. Do you sense envy and resentment?"

For his part, Gil's response was a firm as cast lead: "I haven't encountered such phenomena. I sense only compliments and joy over my success."

I wondered: "Is he alone? Are we talking about one, isolated nut or are most of the Jewish People crazy like him? Are the griping and complaining just exaggerated, without any connection to the reality?

The news reported that in an anti-terrorist operation, an I.D.F. soldier was killed. From the investigation it became clear that he was killed by a stray bullet from his commander during the course of a face-to-face confrontation with demonstrators. The head of the Central Command decided to oust the commander from the army. The response of the bereaved parents was very unexpected. Or perhaps expected? The question is what you expect.

Here is the Ynet news report:

VICTIM'S FAMILY TO ARMY CHIEF:
DON'T FIRE COMMANDER:

The family of first-sergeant Noam Adin Rechter Levi hosted the army's Chief-of-Staff in their home, and asked him not to oust the officer from whose weapon came the stray bullet that killed their son.

Ten days after the death of first sergeant Noam Adin Rechter Levi at Bir Zayit by Ramallah, his family met yesterday with Chief-of-Staff Major General Gabi Ashkenazi and asked him not to oust from the army the officer from whose weapon the fatal bullet was fired. Last Tuesday it had been decided to oust the company deputy commander and to discharge him from the army, following the investigation.

The Chief-of-Staff arrived at the family's home in Mitzpe Netufa. During the meeting, the family addressed the Chief-of-Staff and remarked that they harbor no rancor towards the deputy commander who was with their son during the incident. They said that even if the officer erred in the way he handled the incident, it was wrong to oust him from the army and other steps should be taken against him if necessary. Major General Ashkenazi responded that he would examine the debriefing and act accordingly.

Last week, the officer visited the bereaved family, who received him warmly and pointed out to him that they feel no anger over what occurred.

Their son had been killed due to a tragic error and they could have cast blame. Even the army had ruled against the officer who shot in error. They could have been bitter against everyone.

Yet they chose to be as strong as cast lead; to take a positive approach. They chose to embrace and to love. Their approach was so humane, so Jewish. I wondered: From whence the strength of parents who have lost their son, not through the enemy but through an error, to feel this way and to transmit such warmth to the person who killed their son?

I wondered, and deep inside the answer became increasingly clear. In the previous four months I had seen enormous strength within the entire Jewish People – soldiers, families, physicians and commanders, new immigrants from Russia and veteran citizens, enormous strengths that teach us that the Jewish People are not in an abject state, but rather live and endure.

"A Coincidence"

One of our yeshiva's teachers referred me to an article by Kobi Niv about a film from the Internet dealing with miracles from the Gulf War, from eight years of qassam rockets falling on the South, and from Operation Cast Lead. The film shows numerous media clips in which broadcasters spoke of the great miracle involved in many qassam rockets falling without injuring anyone. In an article entitled, "No miracle happened to us," the writer made light of the movie and called upon the media to stop using the word "miracle". "For us secular," he wrote, "this term has no religious significance. Rather, it connotes a strange coincidence."

And I thought to myself, "'Strange coincidence'! What a lovely, evasive definition! For example, if, each day for three days, a bag with 200 shekels were placed by my front door, and I explained it as "strange coincidence", what would people think of me?

One Friday Night, we had just made kiddush and were enjoying our meal in the home of our daughter who lives in Eilat. Aharon and Tzvia were in their home in Kedumim. Aharon had just recently been allowed to start spending Sabbaths at home. Aharon felt a liquid starting to drip out of one of the scars on his head. After attempts to stop the flow, it was decided to go to the hospital. Once again he was driving on Shabbat. Driving on Shabbat to participate in the military operation had been permissible because the entire country faced danger. This time he was driving with Tzvia on Shabbat because there was a chance his own life was in danger.

At Beilinson Hospital, it turned out that bacteria had attached itself to his skull and begun to infect the skull bone that had been restored just a month before. "There's no choice," the surgeon explained. "We've got to operate."

We had a very bad feeling. Were we regressing? The surgeon sensed the mood and he said, "Don't forget where we were and where we are now. You could have been left a vegetable with your wife unable to remarry. Thank G-d, there's no danger here whatsoever."

A person has to plan out his life, but to know that all is subject to change. On Saturday Night we flew to Tel Aviv. We were sure we were headed for home in Karnei Shomron, yet the cellular rang and Aharon informed us that he was in Beilinson.

"What happened?" we asked. "I've got puss coming out of my head, and there's probably an infection of the bone that was restored a month ago," Aharon explained.

We landed and raced to the hospital. The next day Aharon was brought in for his operation. "We'll open up and see what's going on inside," said the surgeon. During the operation, they decided to remove the skull bone that had been put back. Bacteria that existed only in hospitals had decided to take up residence in Aharon's head. There was an infection, and the bone had to be treated.

We had already gotten used to seeing Aharon with his head

intact or almost intact. Now, it wasn't so simple for us to see him with an indentation in his head once more. And altogether, until the moment before the operation, Aharon had been in a wonderful mood and felt healthy in every way. As I have already said, not everything visible to the eye is what is really happening beneath the surface.

In every moment in life, one can ask: What is my gaze focused on now? On the one hand, Aharon was living, breathing, talking and functioning on his own, and there hadn't been one doctor who would have been willing to wager that Aharon's condition would be so good. On the other hand, the difficulties were obvious. Aharon would have to undergo more and more operations, and things were less good than they had been. Yet is there anyone whose situation is clear and certain? Even when one has a positive perspective and focuses on the cup that is half full, dealing with such an injury is no simple matter at all. I prayed that this descent as well would lead to an ascent, just as the world is darkest before the dawn.

Monday Morning, Aharon began to recuperate from the operation. It was hard to see him once more missing part of his skull bone. His head looked half normal and healthy, and half missing. Aharon was in pain, and we were all very upset. How were we supposed to digest this new/old situation?

Yet gradually we got back to our old selves, to that positive, optimistic approach that is so energizing. More precisely, Aharon was the first to restore us to that positive perspective. "Come on, everything's going to be fine," he said, pulling us along with him.

Thursday a meeting was scheduled in Tel HaShomer Hospital to discuss whether or not to change Aharon from a hospital Rehab patient to an outpatient. In Aharon's condition, would the meeting be held? Would he be able to leave Beilinson four days after an operation in which much of his skull had been removed?

By Tuesday Morning Aharon seemed to be recuperating. He was smiling, joking and making clear to the physician that on Thursday there was a medical board meeting at Tel HaShomer. "I'm going to that meeting, come what may. I feel good and there'll be no problem with my getting there." The doctor already knew

Aharon, and he told me that even if Aharon was not discharged on Thursday, they would let him appear before the meeting in Tel HaShomer. "Where does he get his strength from?" the doctor wondered.

Thursday Morning, Aharon was discharged from Beilinson Hospital. He would continue treatment at Tel HaShomer and at home. We arrived for the meeting at 11 AM, precisely as planned. Aharon's doctor in Rehabilitation began with her summary: "Aharon arrived here at Tel HaShomer three months ago with multi-systemic injuries to his eye, hand, mouth and jaw, as well as a head injury. He didn't eat, couldn't swallow, couldn't speak and couldn't walk independently. Today, he can do everything."

"Praise be to G-d for He is good!" I whispered.

"Where does his strength come from? How do you explain his progress?" the head nurse Regina asked me.

I didn't respond. I had considered this question many times during the past four months. Was it faith, optimism, inner fortitude, focusing on the good, or perhaps sanitizing reality and denying the bad?

Often I had considered that perhaps my denial and my thinking about a better future were what gave me the strength to deal with sights so difficult for a parent to see.

It was decided that on Sunday in a week, May 23, four-and-a-half months after the injury, Aharon would leave the Rehabilitation Department and become an outpatient.

From the meeting, I drove to Rabbi Firer. For two weeks, already, he had been consulting with two plastic surgeons abroad about the operation that would reconstruct Aharon's nose and repair his head. In actual fact, those operations would create a new nose for Aharon. They considered bringing the surgeon to Israel, but Rav Firer explained that it would be better for Aharon to undergo the operations abroad.

I left that meeting and drove to Karnei Shomron. It was 4:45 PM. A radio program was starting called "Search for Relatives", hosted by Yaron Enosh. An amazing tale was told. A Jew named Tzafrir Carmeli related that he was at the "Chain of the Generations" Museum in Jerusalem. You enter a long, dark, winding corridor. On the sides, on layers of special glass, are recorded names from Jewish history, from Abraham to the present.

"The guide encouraged us to lay our palms on the glass in order to take in the atmosphere of the place. I am an obedient person, and I did what he suggested. Yet after some time I got the idea and I stopped laying my hand on the glass. I continued walking along the glass panel and suddenly felt the need to place my hands on the glass once more. I put my hand down, and between my fingers I saw the name "Tzafrir." I removed my hand and saw that the full name was "Tzafrir Carmeli". I was astounded. I am a very rational person, but at that moment I stopped being rational. Obviously, I started investigating who this person was with the same name as I. I discovered that he was a fighter in the Harel Brigade who was killed in the fighting at Castel during the War of Independence."

They interviewed the late Tzafrir Carmeli's sister on the air. In that conversation it turned out that the identical name had been the result of an identical process within two families in different generations: the desire to take on an Israeli name and to express one's love of the Land. "Carmeli, named after Mount Carmel", had brought two families to the same name. How does the saying go? "A strange coincidence".

"Blessed is He who creates man."

Thursday, May 21, was Jerusalem Day, which had began the previous evening with ceremonies marking the forty-second year of Jerusalem's liberation. In the media were all the regular debates over the unification of Jerusalem and the Six Day War.

In the newspaper *Ha'Aretz*, Nadav Shragai wrote:

""At the end of the day, when all the speeches are over, the Palestinian State – and with it the State of Israel – will rise or fall over Jerusalem . . . The main thing is to tell the Jewish story of Jerusalem again and again. It is a story without parallel. Without Jerusalem, there would have been no rebirth to this people precisely here in Eretz Yisrael. We must tell it without tiring, without blinking, and without letting ourselves be confused either by those in our midst who err and lead astray or by those who threaten us from without."

I thought to myself, "How can it be that so many people do not know this richly Jewish story? How can so many be in error?

Library Friday Morning

I was reminded of an interview with Microsoft founder Bill Gates. He was asked why, in his view, so many Israelis take up important positions in his company. He said the Israelis are in a constant state of agitation, aspiring for more. They don't suffice with what there is. This makes them leaders in Hi-tech. In other words, the very trait that leads the Jewish People to quarrelling and saber rattling is the positive trait that brings us to achievements in all realms of life.

I thought back to my first trip to Switzerland. Ben Gurion Airport was a chaotic maelstrom. People were running around, talking in a loud voice and even shouting. They were entering the duty-free shops and coming out with their arms full.

The landing at the Zurich airport left me in shock. Such silence reigned that you could hear a pin drop. Everyone was walking slowly. I waited outside the airport for my relative to pick me up. Minutes passed until he arrived, and I bore witness to a scene no Israeli would believe. People were standing, waiting for a cab. They weren't waiting in the street, nor on the curb. Neither did they wave their arms to hail a cab. Five people stood next to one another about a meter-and-a-half from the curb, waiting, without saying a word and without an extraneous movement. The moment a cab stopped, the person in line got in, and after that the next person in line, and so forth. All this happened quietly, calmly, tranquilly. The arrival of the car that had come to pick me up broke my thoughts. I got into the car and immediately asked, "Have I arrived in Paradise?"

"What happened?" the driver asked. I told him what my eyes had seen. He immediately calmed me down and said, "They have no ambitions but an apartment and a car. Where do you want them to rush to?" We drove through the area of the Zurich train station. Along the sidewalk next to a large park, hundreds of youth were sitting on the ground, busy with other types of "aspirations". They were sniffing and shooting up drugs that cut them off from our world. I got the point.

That day, Jerusalem Day, starting from the morning, we were busy with Aharon's discharge from Rehabilitation and his move to the day clinic, from which he would return home each afternoon. Another phase of Aharon's recovery process was starting. We emptied all the clothing and other items from Aharon's closet.

It was an odd sensation. On the one hand, there was great joy over his marvelous, speedy progress. On the other hand, numerous treatments and complex operations lay ahead.

That evening we were invited to the wedding of Elishama Rein. Elishama, a very good friend of Aharon, exerted considerable pressure on Aharon until he agreed to recite a blessing under the wedding canopy. The Rein family are amongst the builders of the Land, and they also belong to the "bereavement club". Their son, Benaya, was killed in the Second Lebanon War. His tank squad was called "Benaya's force", and it was charged with rescuing forces that found themselves in a tight spot. Benaya, the commander, grew up in our town, Karnei Shomron, making him what the media calls a "National-Religious settler". His tank was manned by four soldiers, who belonged to the "Shelach" Battalion from the Armor Brigade. Those four, who symbolize more than anything else the pigments and complexity of Israeli society, were enclosed in one box of steel to fight together for the Jewish People.

Here is what appeared in the press about the human make-up of the tank when it was decided to award a citation for courage in battle, and especially regarding three heroic rescue missions:

One of the famous stories of Brigade 401 during the Second Lebanon War was the story of "Benaya's force". Benaya's Force was a tank crew from Battalion 46, which was pieced together by Benaya Rein. The crew consisted of Major Benaya Rein, First Sergeant Alex Bonirovitz, a Russian immigrant, First Sergeant Adam Goren from Kibbutz Ma'abarot and First Sergeant Uri Grossman, son of the author David Grossman. Benaya was a company commander without a company, so he gathered together the fighters at the start of the war. The crew, called "Benaya's Force" due to its lack of a connection to any other, engaged in rescue operations, and in many instances saved fighters inside Lebanon. One time, Benaya's Force rescued eight Engineering Corps fighters from a damaged armored engineering vehicle under fire.

On their way to one rescue attempt, the crew's tank suffered a direct hit from an advanced anti-tank missile, and all four were killed on the spot. After the war, the crew was awarded a general's citation for the courage and self-sacrifice they exhibited during the battles and rescue missions."

At Elishama's wedding, everyone danced before him and his bride, ushering them under the *chuppa*, the wedding canopy. Suddenly I saw Gabi Ashkenazi, the Chief-of-Staff, arrive at the wedding. He approached me and he said, "I want a hug." We hugged and chatted. The head of the most special army in the world knew the father of one wounded soldier out of many, hugged him and chatted with him without any partitions between them, without any of the trappings of honor and glory, with naturalness and simplicity. Fortunate the nation with him for its Chief-of-Staff.

Aharon was called upon to recite one of the seven blessings recited under the chuppa. He ascended the stage and recited, "Blessed are You O L-rd, Creator of Man." Tears flowed from my eyes. Had "Somebody" directed this blessing precisely to Aharon, or was this a "strange coincidence"? "The Creator of man" had preserved Aharon's form despite his mortal injury. He had preserved his psychological and spiritual form, and more or less his external form as well.

Stories from Jerusalem Day, the Six Day War and from "Benaya's Force" during the Second Lebanon War circulated through the wedding hall. The differences between the Six Day War and the Second Lebanon War cried out. During the former, the nation was united around the justness of their cause and their mutual commitment. During the latter, divisiveness and doubts over the justness of the cause took up a major part of our lives.

Here is something amazing: On Army Radio they interviewed the commander of Hamas regarding Operation Cast Lead. He was asked, "Why did the Hamas fighters abandon their positions in Gaza?" Everyone knew they had prepared significant fortifications and "surprises" for the I.D.F. So when put to the test, why did many of them pick up their tails and run, allowing the I.D.F. to advance without ever facing a real battle.

The Hamas man answered, "We thought Israeli society had disintegrated, such that the soldiers would fall into our hands like ripe fruit. Yet when we understood that the Jewish people are united and believe in the war, we understood that G-d was with them."

"Interesting," I thought. "In the Six Day War they left their shoes behind and fled, and they did so in Cast Lead as well. Yet this didn't happen in the Yom Kippur War or in the Second Lebanon War. Can it be that only in situations of unity and faith in the justness of our path are we privileged to see that G-d fights for our side?"

Ezra LaMarpei

My cell phone awakened me: "Hello, this is Kalman from *Ezra LaMarpei*. After the Shavuot Holiday there's going to be an evening honoring Rabbi Firer and his *Ezra LaMarpe* organization. I would like to ask: Would you and Aharon agree to address us that evening?"

I spoke to Aharon about the request. Fulfilling that request was no easy matter for him. Moving from being a man of quiet action to one whose power is in his speech was doubly hard. It involved both the physical difficulty of speaking, as well as his becoming an orator.

"We have no choice," he said. "We've got thank Rav Firer," he said. Rav Firer had helped us with all our medical dealings regarding Aharon.

The event was being held five months after the injury. I arrived alone and waited for Tzvia and Aharon in front of Tel Aviv's Charles Bronfman Auditorium. Thousands of people were crowding around the entrance to gain admittance. There were men with head coverings and men without, women dressed modestly and women dressed as though headed for the beach. I did something not so nice. I stopped passersby and asked, "Do you know what is scheduled for this evening?" and all answered identically and decisively, "no".

"So why did you come?" I asked them. This is an important point, because tickets were expensive, starting from 300 shekels for a cheap ticket, up to thousands of shekels for an expensive ticket. Aharon, Tzvia and I received tickets from the organization worth 700 shekels each.

What would induce all these people to pay such high prices for an event where they don't know what is planned? If they decided to make a donation, let them donate. But why bother coming to an auditorium for blind programming?

"What do you mean?" they looked at me in puzzlement. "We came to say thank you to this wonderful man and to aid his activities. We don't care what is planned. Let it be some speeches and songs and be done with it."

Aharon and Tzvia arrived. Aharon hastened to find a corner where he could unhook the antibiotic that was attached to him twice a day since the violent bacteria had attacked his skull. He sat down on a chair in a natural manner, and like a pro, opened one valve, closed a second, cleansed a third, and he was done. We found our assigned seats. The Israeli entertainer Tzvika Hadar was the M.C. The first performer to appear, singer Yehoram Gaon, turned to Rav Firer and said, "All the performers appearing here are doing so voluntarily, as a mark of esteem for your work. I know I get a brownie point in heaven when I help you, and that is my reward."

Minister Yitzchak Herzog rose to speak. He spoke with amazement about Rav Firer, a man whose whole life is devoted to the public. "Even on the Sabbath he answers the phone, since we are talking about lives being in danger," stressed the minister.

Tzvika Hadar invited Aharon up on stage. In a tremulous voice, he said that before Aharon spoke, we would see a short film clip. The clip dealt chiefly with the ceremony at which Aharon was promoted to first lieutenant. I was seeing this film for the first time, like a spectator from the side. My tears flowed with joy and excitement. The clip ended and Tzvika Hadar said, "I am honored to call upon the hero of Israel, Aharon Karov."

The classification "hero of Israel" vis-a-vis Aharon was heard over and over. Did they mean it? Why? The entire audience stood on its feet and roared, for three minutes, four minutes, and maybe more. It was hard not to get excited.

We know that all of Israel's soldiers are heroes, and Aharon, who became famous, is just one of them. But there you are: Five months after the injury, the Jewish People still remembered Aharon and were excited to see him. As I said, the Jewish People are excited and impressed by people who consecrate their lives, wholly or partially, to the public welfare.

Instances of this excitement did not cease, surprising us, each time anew, with their intensity:

The next day we were driving to the Vehicular Registration Bureau in Holon. Just the thought of our going to that place, so jam-packed with people, made me shudder. We approached the window to which we had been referred, in order to arrange Aharon's driver's license with the new status of "Disabled Veteran". We took a number and we stood on the side. Suddenly one of the people waiting in line before us approached us and asked, "What is your number?"

"Sixty-three", I replied. "Hand over your number!" the man cried, and before I understood what was happening, he stretched out his hand and took the number. He then presented me with his own number. I looked and saw the number "fifty-two". I looked at the digital screen over the clerk and saw the number "fifty-one". I understood that a Jew had given me his turn, and I tried to resist.

"Excuse me! In this country, they still show heroes a bit of respect," he retorted forcefully, in a tone that made clear that there was no chance that he could be dissuaded. I saw that all the other people waiting in line were pumping their heads in agreement. When we finished our turn, I looked back and saw that the others had allowed the one who had given up his turn to approach the window. What an inspiration!

Aharon phoned me and asked, "Dad, where in the Bible do we find the parable of the poor man's lamb?" How overjoyed I was to hear Aharon dealing with such topics! That famous parable

(II Samuel 12) deals with a wealthy, covetous man with much sheep and cattle who takes away a poor man's only lamb.

It was now precisely five months since the injury. On the one hand, this was almost an eternity. I had almost forgotten those first days. On the other hand, it was really only five months since that awful injury.

On the one hand, what a wonderful situation we were in. Aharon was himself again. He was the same Aharon as before the injury, with the same desires, reactions, style and mode of speech. On the other hand, he still had a lot of medical treatments to undergo, and his speech was not what it had been. Several major operations still lay ahead as well.

Aharon was spending three to four days a week in rehabilitation until the afternoon, and then he would drive to the Yeshiva in Karnei Shomron to study Torah. Who would have believed we'd be privileged to see him doing this just five months after the injury!

Everyone who saw Aharon returning to normal after the injury tried his best to explain the phenomenon. Some put their finger on Aharon's willpower, others stressed his supportive family, and still others mentioned the devoted physicians.

One of the many gifts we received following Aharon's injury was the book "*Teluyim BaRuach*" [English: Hanging in the Wind/ Dependent on the Spirit] by Eli Ziv. Ziv was wounded during the Six Days War as a young paratrooper, and for years he felt drawn to assisting with rehabilitating the wounded. In the book he tells the story of several severely wounded soldiers from Israel's wars, and he shows how they all coped. The common thread to all the stories is the wounded soldier's will power and the education each received at home from a young age.

I, too, talk a lot about a strong spirit and a mighty will. Yet during those first five months, I saw severely wounded soldiers whose spirits were not strong, and yet they still improved. Aharon always had a smile on his face, and always said, "Everything's all right." Some injured are the opposite. They have a constant look of anger and their eyes show constant suffering. Yet they, too, advance beyond a state in which the assessment of all the physicians is "a vegetable at most". And with great sadness I have also seen parents full of motivation, whose sons continue to be vegetables, with no improvement in their situation for many months.

Doubtless, will power and a supportive environment have an enormous influence on the injured soldier's rehabilitation. Yet the starting point is elsewhere entirely. It is above us; beyond our understanding. As our sages said, "If all the wise men of the nations assembled together to create a single mosquito, they could not infuse it with a soul".

The Human Brain

Twenty-five years ago I visited the home of Professor Feurstein, a rare, colorful personality in our parts, a very elderly man, with a perpetual beret perched on his head. With a penetrating gaze, he speaks pleasantly until angered.

For me, Professor Feuerstein is first and foremost the father of my friend Rafi. Here is an amazing person who fifty years ago came up with two revolutionary claims, and the Israeli establishment rejected and even mocked him. Outside Israel, his approach has been recognized for many years, while in our holy land only in recent years have they begun to relate to him seriously. He dealt with the human brain and its functioning. In those days, scientists were certain the brain was a technical apparatus that could not be changed or influenced. In their opinion, if particular brain cells in the human brain had been damaged, they were irreparable and irreplaceable. Professor Feurstein came out vociferously against that claim, arguing that there is no organ of the human body that is as alterable as the brain.

His second, bolder claim was that when we challenge the brain and make it think, it leads to the production of neurons and the regeneration of human brain cells. In simple words, it is not matter that sustains spirit, but the opposite: spirit sustains matter. Professor Feuerstein developed methods for working with individuals suffering from Down's Syndrome and other forms of brain damage. His successes are known the world over. In many countries films have been produced about him and about his method.

I read the American psychiatrist, Norman Doidge's book, *The Brain that Changes Itself*. He, as well, described the derision he suffered when he was starting out, when he attempted alongside other researchers, to prove through research that the brain is flexible and changes. These men may have been mocked, but their words – albeit in less strident tones – we heard in every hospital in which Aharon received treatment: "We know that the brain is very elastic and changes take place in it, at least during the first year after the injury" . . . "With proper work, dormant cells will replace those damaged in the injury".

We experience these changes every moment. Based on where Aharon's brain was injured, he wasn't supposed to be able to talk, but he was talking plenty. His right-side functioning was supposed to have been damaged, but that was not the case.

We entered Professor Feurstein's office in Jerusalem with Aharon. I was very excited to see him. It was as though time had stood still. He was approaching ninety, but his appearance was as it had been. He was as alert and vibrant as he had been twenty-five years before.

He addressed Aharon, saying, "I went over your file, and I'm sure you are aware that you constitute a great miracle. I'm really excited to meet you."

He asked questions, examined Aharon's medical file and whispered something unintelligible to his assistant. Afterwards he said, "You've got to realize how important it is to challenge the brain, particularly with new things. Novelty has the ability to influence the brain more than anything else. Learn a new Talmudic text, study a new profession. If you're not computer savvy, take a computer course. Every mental stimulus to the brain creates neurons and renews cells." And he added, "Novelty and study will help the miracle to endure."

The truth is that we had heard this from the director of the Rehabilitation Department as well, a Russian immigrant who said, "I tell religious Jews who have been injured to study Talmud with a partner. That's the best thing for them." She had said this without explaining herself, and I had wondered, "Are we consulting a medical expert or hearing a lecture on faith and mysticism?

Yet more than anything, I pondered a situation in which such innovative people are not properly appreciated. Many times, the establishment apparatus and habit override innovation and truth. It is easy for people to remain in a place they are familiar with and not to be exposed to innovations that are liable to offer them a new look at life.

On our way back I recalled our lawyer, who was assisting us in everything concerning Aharon's status in the Defense Ministry. She and her husband, both lawyers, are far from religious observance and from the religious public, but as far as I am concerned, they are true saints. They help many disabled veterans in all sorts of ways. They are good people with a warm, Jewish heart. I called to ask how she was. Her husband answered and said that Sigal could not come to the phone. "How are you both?" I asked. "Very well!" came the couple's regular answer. Five minutes later Sigal called back. "My father passed away several minutes ago, and I was not free to answer. How are you?"

Some people, even in their hardest moments, think about others and are free to give them a moment.

Two days after the funeral, I went to pay a condolence call. We talked about many varied things. At some point her husband asked me, "Why do we need to preserve the Hebrew date and not use a date that most of the world uses? Must every tradition and custom be preserved?"

I explained to them the difference in values and substance between the solar calendar used by most of the world, and the lunar calendar used by the Jewish People. "The sun symbolizes set laws of nature that never change. As King Solomon wrote, 'There is nothing new under the sun' (Ecclesiastes 1:9). The moon, by contrast, is renewed each month. Our lives revolve around change, around renewing and improving ourselves all the time." As I spoke, I recalled Professor Feuerstein's explanation about the brain's power of renewal and his position that it is forbidden for brain-impaired people to stop trying, versus the approach, found in many rehabilitation wards, that blunts ambitions and suffices with restoring the patient to a technical ability to function.

I explained further, "Moreover, the moon symbolizes humility. It takes the light from the sun and passes it on to us. This involves renewal and innovation, but with great humility. That is our path."

The next morning, I walked slowly to the yeshiva. An ambulance screamed as it left our town, setting out eastward for the town of Kedumim. A routine sight. After about ten minutes, I received an SMS: "Big ruckus by the caravan of the Karov family in Kedumim." Alarmed, I called Aharon's cell phone, and Tzvia answered. "Something has happened to Aharon. He's lost consciousness and the ambulance team is treating him. We'll soon be setting out for the hospital."

Boom!!!

It's hard to receive a message like that. We were feeling like we're on the rise, and suddenly, a fall. What great humility you need in face of the reality, and in face of the Master-of-the-Universe in order to accept the reality and not sink into melancholy. Suddenly you begin to understand that with an injury like Aharon's, there can be more complications that you haven't thought about. It's good that you don't think about them.

Aharon was anesthetized, photographs were taken and tests performed to diagnose what had caused the episode. It turned out that Aharon had undergone a sort of epileptic fit that often occurs to people with damaged brains. Everyone hoped it was a one-time occurrence. Three days later, Aharon returned to rehabilitation as an outpatient at Tel HaShomer. Thank G-d, there was no infection or internal bleeding involved, but rather a familiar phenomenon with brain injuries, and certainly with people who had shrapnel that had penetrated their skulls and remained there.

"I must point out that even after what he just went through he's still a great miracle," said Dr. Agaronova, head of Rehabilitation. She, too, reminded us to look at the whole picture and to focus our glance on the cup that is half full.

Friday the telephone rang. One of my rabbinic mentors would scrupulously call me every third week to ask how Aharon was doing. I told him about the attitude of Professor Feuerstein and the head of Rehabilitation to Talmud study. As was his way, he put matters precisely. Talmud study is important and influences our brains, not just because it sharpens our minds but also, and chiefly, because it constitutes the word of the Living G-d. When we learn Torah, we attach ourselves to the Source of Life, and we are thus revitalized with new energy and life forces. When someone studies Talmud, he is not renewing his energies solely through his own efforts. Such renewal cannot occur without his attaching himself to the One who brings death and restores life.

I continued reading *The Brain that Changes Itself*, which brings together all the research proving that it is possible to alter the brain. In one chapter the author writes, "It is not yet known to us precisely how our thoughts foment changes in the brain structure, yet today it is clear that they do make such changes, and the concrete dividing line Descartes drew between the spirit and the mind is cracking."

Part IV | One Step Backwards,
Two Steps Forward

Ups and Downs

It was after Tisha Be'Av, the day on which both Temples were destroyed. The Second Temple was destroyed slightly under two thousand years ago due to groundless hatred.

Tisha Be'Av is also Aharon's birthday. We celebrated a non-conventional party with him. On that day, we understood and sensed that Aharon had been born twice. Not everyone is privileged in that way.

Tisha Be'Av Night it was announced that a masked man had shot in all directions at the Tel-Aviv Youth Center. A boy and girl were killed, and about ten more were wounded. Here was hatred for its own sake, and adopting the role of the ideologue, judge and executioner. As usual, the news reported traffic accidents and twelve fatalities during the last week, as well as embezzlement in Israel and abroad, and more stabbings of youth in clubs.

Was this the same Jewish People I had encountered during the past six months? Are there two peoples here, or perhaps one crazy people, with ups and downs?

Can it be that a soldier who one day risked his life for the nation and the country would the very next day stab someone for talking rudely with his girlfriend or for taking a parking spot?

Unfortunately, but, to the same degree, fortunately, the answer is: yes! One day a person can be the greatest saint, and the next day the worst sinner. It is man's job to educate himself so his negative impulse can be bridled and directed towards positive, beneficial purposes. We seem to have no profound, systematic, educational method for uncovering positive traits and giving reign to our good impulses. That's why we see such terrible evil. Yet the positive traits stamped deep within us occasionally peek out from between the cracks.

Immediately after the Second Temple's destruction, the greatest sage of the Mishna, Rabbi Akiva, was walking with several colleagues, themselves great Torah luminaries, and they saw a fox emerging from the Holy of Holies, a harsh sight indeed. The Land of Israel was where the Jewish People had lived as a nation, and the Temple Mount within it was where they would gather together as friends to greet the Divine Presence. Precisely that place was destroyed, and foxes strolled within. Rabbi Akiva's colleagues wept when they saw that awful sight, but Rabbi Akiva laughed. Laughter expresses the power to overcome difficulties. We, too, often laughed as we spent time in hospitals with Aharon. It was a laughter that came from deep within, and it gave us the strength to carry on.

Rabbi Akiva had not gone crazy when he laughed. He was teaching them two things: First, the loftiest reality can descend to the fathomless depths. There are no guarantees to either man or society. One day you can be down low, and the next day up high, and vice versa. Second, everyone can choose how to ponder reality. A generous perspective will accustom you to seeing the possibilities of rebuilding and rebirth even in times of crisis. Rabbi Akiva was telling his colleagues that although the reality was harsh and painful, he understood that the destruction bore within it the potential of redemption and rebuilding, precisely like the pains of childbirth.

Unfortunately, a soldier who is moved from deep within him to run like a lion into battle for the sake of his brothers, is also liable to run to smash his brother's skull over a foolish argument. Man and society must understand the forces operating within us in order to utilize them as a catalyst for building, and not as a sledgehammer for destroying. And I think that cutting oneself off from one's roots, to one degree or another, is what leads us to direct our inner strengths in negative directions. As Rav Kook wrote:

"If something is wrong with the branches, we've got to examine the roots. Our chief effort must be to ensure the robust state of the roots."

Waiting for a Nose

Six months had passed since the injury. For two months already we had been investigating where it would be best to perform the reconstructive surgery on Aharon's nose. This was not regular plastic surgery, but science fiction. Aharon had no nose. Tissue, fat and much else would have to be transplanted in order to reconstruct his nose. It would almost emerge *ex nihilo*.

Rabbi Firer undertook to investigate on our behalf all the methods and possibilities, and to obtain the advice of physicians the world over to decide what was best. In our little country, there are one or two cases per year of this sort of nose injury, if that. Hence the main investigative effort focused on abroad.

The truth is that a few of us had gotten used to Aharon's appearance without a nose. He generally went around with a fake nose made of cork, attached with special glue, and brought in from the United States. Sometimes he wore a bandage, and at home he made due without any disguise. At first his appearance seemed ghastly. Yet after a while you got used to it. After all, man is not his nose. He is a composite of his personality, desires, reactions and behavior. What place does the appearance of the nose have in all of that?

Maybe he didn't need reconstructive surgery at all, I wondered. Perhaps it was expected of us, but were the operations actually superfluous? Had Aharon's capacity for understanding been harmed, we could never have gotten used to that. We would constantly feel the injury and be sorrowful over it. But his nose?

Rabbi Firer called: "Come on over. I think I've found the best physician for Aharon." I arrived at the offices of Rabbi Firer's *Ezra LaMarpe* organization. He told me about Dr. Friedrich Menick of

Arizona, an expert in reconstructive surgery of the face and nose. In his letter, Dr. Menick explained the need for a series of three to four operations to achieve optimal results.

"Arizona is at the end of the world," I said to myself, and I asked Rav Firer whether it was worth leaving the Land of Israel for these operations. "Aharon needs the most attractive appearance possible. Surely, 'a man's wisdom is enhanced by his countenance' (Ecclesiastes 8:1). That will influence how people see him, and how he sees himself."

Deep inside, I was not assuaged. I continued to carry on an inner debate. Part of me asked, "Surely you are a believer in perfection, in the powerful link between body and the soul; matter and spirit. Why are you undecided?" Another part answered, "Operations involve dangers and pain. Is it worth it just for a nose?"

We were waiting to receive a date from the physician regarding when the operations could start. The family was constantly asking, "When will we have a date?" and I was thinking, "It's all in G-d's hands."

The very moment the rumors began about our going to Arizona for surgery, the phone calls began non-stop from Israel and abroad. "I've got family in Arizona. I can ask them to put you up." A Knesset member from the Kadima party informed me that his cousin was "well connected" in the United States and would be happy to be of assistance. The father of Yair Shreider, who was Aharon's machine gunner and was likewise injured in that incident, informed me that a good friend of his had told him that his daughter had undergone a series of operations in Arizona with the best reconstructive facial surgeon in the world. "What is the doctor's name?" I asked. "Menick Friedrich," he answered. The father was ready to assist us in Arizona. The rabbi of the town of Yakir called and said the rabbi of Tucson, Arizona, where the hospital is, had informed him that he would put us up and take care of all our needs.

Thursday, almost seven months after the injury, Aharon returned home in the afternoon from treatment, and we, four of the men of our family, set out together for a "nature dip", an old family custom of ours to visit charming nature spots in Israel, to see them, go swimming and come home. We would drive for about an hour-and-a-half through breathtaking scenery, swim for about two hours and return. We had decided to reestablish this custom with Aharon.

We set out at 3:30 PM and drove through the amazing countryside of the Samarian mountain ridge, overlooking the Jordan Valley, until we arrived at Kibbutzim Stream. Kibbutzim Stream is one of the loveliest spots in our little country, and it flows all year long. Over the course of about two kilometers, you can swim and enjoy clean, clear water. We swam and chatted almost without disturbance. Almost every ten minutes another group passed us.

Aharon and I raced each other in the breaststroke, and he won. He was breathing hard, trying to calm his body down. It looked to me as though he couldn't believe the speed and smooth swimming style that he had succeeded in achieving for himself. The attempt at a butterfly stroke, by contrast, was very hard. The arm movements were still hard for him.

We left and started driving home. We decided to stop in Kfar Saba for supper at the "Achla" Restaurant. We seated ourselves and immediately a waitress arrived and took our orders. After about ten minutes a man approached our table, introducing himself as the manager. "I am pleased and excited to have you at our restaurant. I salute you," he said, and left.

During our time at the restaurant, we felt that he wasn't just talking, but was translating his words to actions. Every five minutes a waiter or waitress arrived with a special dish, adding the phrase, "on the house". Towards the end of the meal, a soufflé cake arrived with ice cream, sure enough, on the house. At the end of the meal, we recited the Grace After Meals, thanking G-d for the privilege of dining on the Land's bounties. I asked the waitress for the tab, and she set off for the cash register. When she returned, she announced, "We received instructions that you are not to pay. And thank you very much for eating here." Aharon and I got up together and asked to speak with the owner. The response was, "He's gone, and he asked us to thank you."

While we were still in shock, only starting to understand what had just occurred, one of the diners at the next table approached us. I saw that he was trembling and in tears. "May I shake the hands of the heroes?" It was seven months after the injury, and the Jewish People still remembered, and continued to be excited and to be partners with us.

In the coming days I told many people about our swim competition. Some raised their eyebrows and said, "What? He can *swim*?" while others wondered, "What? He still has limitations?"

By late July, for some reason, we had not yet received a date for the first nose operation. There was a feeling that something was holding up the works. It had taken a long time to decide on a surgeon, and when that was finally decided, the operation date was just not coming.

"It's all from G-d," I told Aharon and his wife. Something "upstairs" is causing the delay. G-d willing, all would be for the best.

August

Late in August, the last day before the Jewish month of Elul, we were on a family vacation. Since a surgery date had not yet been set, we found time to take our customary vacation in the North. At the last moment, our daughter had succeeded in finding guest apartments in the Katzrin field school in the Golan Heights.

We set off for a trip through the enchanting north. There seemed to be a contradiction between appearances and reality. On the surface, the Golan looked parched and yellowed. Under the surface there was flowing water and prodigious life.

We were swimming in a hidden spring when suddenly a group of soldiers from the elite "Egoz" unit popped up. Their officer recognized Aharon. They had been together in officer training.

Towards evening, we arrived at the field school. I went in to the office and announced, "The Karov Family. We ordered rooms." The reception clerk examined the orders ledger and asked, "Excuse me? What is your name?" I repeated, "the Karov Family". He examined the records gravely and said, "I am sorry. There is no such order." After a closer look, it turned out that the order had accidentally been registered for the following week. I was upset, trying to figure out where to take sixteen tired people after a strenuous hike. Where could I now find an alternative spot?

"Dad, smile," I heard Aharon calling towards me. He pulled his lips towards his ears. Due to the stitches in his cheek, he seemed to be in a perpetual smile. He then said, "Dad, don't worry. We'll manage. Smile like me." After a minute or two he approached me and said, "My injury taught me that you've got to be happy with everything you've got."

I was in shock, overwrought with joy, fighting off the tears that sought to cover my eyes and cheeks. This is what Aharon had learned! This is what he says! This is how he behaves! I thought to myself, "What a wonderful preparation for Elul, the month before the High Holy Days! Just to hear such words, and then to hear them specifically from Aharon, was worth the mistaken registration in the Katzrin Field School. And indeed, we found an alternative place to stay in the town of Keshet.

Two days later, my wife and I were at the Israeli Army's Officer Training Academy, where I had been invited to spend Shabbat and to transmit a series of lectures. As we entered the gates of the army base, a chill ran down our spines. The last time we had been there was at Aharon's graduation ceremony from Officer Training. It was a strange feeling. Aharon's role as an officer ceased due to the injury. Eight of the soldiers from Aharon's company were now in officer training. They approached us and asked how he was doing.

The atmosphere that Shabbat astounded me. Hundreds of soldiers came to the talks, some bare-headed and some with head coverings. Some say that the enormous attendance at the talks was due to my being the father of Aharon Karov. During recent months, I had earned a new title, "Aharon's father".

The human material here was excellent and aroused hopes and pride. Before Kiddush on Friday Night, a bare-headed major rose and addressed all the soldiers. He spoke about the week's Torah portion, *Parashat Shoftim*. He surveyed the portion and its ramifications for commanders. At the end of his talk, he turned to the soldiers and he said, "You won't find me in the synagogue, but I recommend to all of you to study the weekly Torah portion. This is our tradition and our heritage, and you can learn a lot from it." I found myself saying once more, "How fortunate we are to have such commanders."

In one of my lectures I spoke about the heroism inherent in self-restraint and self-control. As the Rabbis said, "Who is heroic? He who subdues his passions" (Avot 4:1) I explained that the valor of a soldier advancing in battle begins with the valor of self-restraint. Every soldier in battle overcomes the desire to worry about himself and quashes his fears. It is this self-restraint which allows him to advance. The heroism of the groom who leaves his wedding celebration for battle likewise involves self-control, the ability to put one's personal desires aside for the sake of the entire nation.

The Rabbis said, "There is no happiness like the removal of doubts." At last a date was set for Aharon's first operation in Arizona, November 2, almost a month after the holidays. It was a bit disappointing to have to wait so long, but that's it. The date was known.

Two weeks later it would become clear that our happiness was premature.

Citation

Seven months and three weeks after the injury, the Chief-of-Staff authorized the granting of seven citations to veterans of "Cast Lead". One Thursday Morning we were hit by an avalanche of phone calls from the media. We discovered that two of the citations involved Aharon's rescue.

Here is what I found in one of the I.D.F.'s Internet sites:

"Almost certainly, the story of the miraculous recovery of Second lieutenant Aharon Karov, who had decided to join the battle just one day after his wedding, would not have happened at all if not for the cool-headedness of CAPTAIN (then first lieutenant) MOTTI IFLACH. On Wednesday, January 14, in the course of a paratrooper operation in the Shaati Refugee Camp in the Northern Gaza Strip, troops entered a building. A mine detonated in the proximity of the force injured a number of fighters, among them Second Lieutenant Aharon Karov, who was mortally wounded. First Lieutenant Iflach arrived on the scene, found said victim suffering from severe injuries to his limbs and face, and acted with determination and professionalism to save him, performing a procedure to open the wounded's air passage, under harsh conditions. Lieutenant Iflach's decision to carry out that procedure, and the way he did it under those harsh conditions, led to the wounded man's being saved. Lieutenant Iflach evacuated the wounded man in an armored vehicle and continued to resuscitate him for forty more minutes until they arrived at the helicopter launch pad. Amongst the commission's arguments for his selection: First Lieutenant Iflach demonstrated by his actions devotion to duty, professional valor, determination and cool-headedness.

"Another fighter who took part in saving the life of Second Lieutenant Aharon Karov was MASTER-SERGEANT (RESERVES) ZIV, who was performing his reserve duty as an airborne paramedic of the Air Force's Rescue and Evacuation Unit. Master Sergeant Ziv, after consulting with the airborne physician, and employing determination and professionalism, performed a surgical procedure on the wounded man, inserting a breathing tube through an incision in his throat. All this he did in the midst of an operational helicopter flight. Master Sergeant (reserves) Ziv, who performed the surgical procedure to perfection, while demonstrating great professionalism, and thereby saving the life of Second Lieutenant Karov, will receive a citation from the Base Commander of Tel Nof. Through his actions, Master Sergeant (reserves) Ziv demonstrated devotion to duty, professional valor, determination and cool-headedness."

I read this and was excited by it. Numerous thoughts ran through my head. Once more I recalled Aharon's critical state following the injury. I digested the fact that for so many minutes, they fought for his ability to breath. From within me burst forth the cry, "It is forbidden to despair!" As our sages said, "Even if a sharp sword is pressed against one's throat, one must not despair." We are forbidden to perceive our lives through the confining prism of logic and rationalism. Much of life is irrational and defies explanation. Our life force is stronger, profounder and larger than the force of logic.

On Friday, Ziv, the paramedic who performed the surgery in the helicopter, was interviewed on Radio Channel 2. He humbly spoke about his citation going to the entire unit in which he served. "We train, and our job is to do our utmost to help every wounded soldier," he said modestly. Following the broadcast we chatted. I thanked him and blessed him on his having received the citation. And how did he respond? He quickly changed the subject to talk about Aharon and our family.

"I learned a lot about your family and about how you coped, and how you are continuing to cope, with the injury. I have learned a lot from that." He spoke with great passion. One might say: the citation didn't raise his nose. It exalted his spirit. We set up to meet.

Right after my conversation with Ziv, I saw a Torah message in the Ynet Internet site regarding the Torah portion of *Ki Tavo*, written by the Israeli actor Nati Ravitz. He was talking about the verse, "Cursed is he who misdirects a blind person on his way" (Deuteronomy 27:18). Ravitz wrote, "Whoever remains passive when he sees the needs and difficulties of others, may think he is looking out for himself, but the opposite is the case. Worrying about others increase's one's own worth and vitality. Some people won't help the other lest the other grab their place. That is a mistaken fear. Quite the contrary, helping others magnifies one's individual strengths and one's life then encompasses much more."

I was simultaneously privileged to learn a lesson in the spirit of Rav Kook about our duty to the public good and about recognizing that man is part of a larger whole, and I was further privileged to see and hear these ideas embodied in Ziv, who lives this way. I felt a great affinity for these two men. Presumably, neither followed the same educational track that I did. They did not learn in Yeshivat Mercaz HaRav Kook, where I learned. Yet you can see, despite the great distance in education and in the way their lives have developed, we've got so much in common as far as the deeper content of life.

Whenever news broadcasts try to make me feel the difference

between Jews, reality cries out, "Don't be tempted to see only the differences!" As already stated, not everything visible on the surface indicates what is really happening beneath the surface. I ponder the Talmudic concept of "light and darkness mingling together", but I have the feeling that the light is much stronger, despite attempts to emphasize the darkness.

One day I was about to start a talk to a group of people planning the establishment of a Torah core group in the "Hadar" Neighborhood of Haifa. An older man approached me. The positioning of his head covering testified that it wasn't always there on his head. He handed me an envelope and said, "My wife spoke with you several months ago. It was I who promised to make a contribution if your son came home to his wife."

I began my talk. Occasionally my eyes fell on the man and I tried to recall as I spoke who his wife was and what it was all about. Only after I finished my lecture did I recall.

Sure enough, several months before, a woman had called, introduced herself and said she was from Haifa. She said that her husband was irreligious, and that in a discussion between them over whether prayer would help Aharon or not, he had promised that if they helped and Aharon came home to live with his wife, he would donate money. He had promised, and now, several months later, he had kept his promise.

Two days later, I was driving to the resort village of the Soldier's Club in Givat Olga. The scenery was breathtaking. There was a strip of beach extending from the village as though it had been taken from pictures or photographs from other lands. The sea was tranquil and its color was a deep blue. There was a strong sense of nature in its pristine, primeval state.

"I wanted to tell you that the story of your son provided us with great encouragement. It truly brought us back from the dead." I heard these words, but I had a hard time digesting them. These words were being uttered after a talk I had given to bereaved families at the resort village. The speaker's son was a soldier murdered by terrorists while on a hike. I asked myself, "How could our story encourage or revive bereaved parents?" I asked this, and I had a hard time answering my question.

When I was invited to address bereaved families, I asked whether it was right and proper for me to do that. After all, I had been fortunate – my son was getting stronger and returning to life, whereas that hadn't happened for them. Wouldn't my talk be like rubbing salt into their wounds? The answer was, "The families requested that you talk."

As soon as I finished talking, another couple approached me and told me a riveting story. One of their sons had taken part in the struggle against the Gush Katif expulsion. In that struggle, he had debated a reservist who had volunteered to expel settlers. That's right! An idealist against the settlers of Judea and Samaria. The debate created a bond between the two. That's right! Precisely through the debate, the bond was created. Two weeks after Aharon was injured, the reservist who had volunteered to expel Jews called their son and said, "This story is giving me no rest. I want to understand what is this faith of yours and of Aharon's family." They concluded the story in tears: "Today, he keeps the Sabbath and wears tzitzit and is undergoing a process of coming closer, accompanied by our son."

As I have already said, the way a person looks in his daily life is no indicator of what is happening deep inside. I half asked and half said, "How can one story move so many people? What brings together and attracts so many different types of people to a story about one boy wounded in a military operation?"

At the end of the story the husband said, "I am closing up a book store in Petach Tikva that belonged to my father. Tell Aharon that he can come and pick books to take home." Aharon has a great love of holy books. That disease presumably was passed on to him as an inheritance from his father, who has the same addiction. I called Aharon and I told him about the meeting and the offer to select books, and he unhesitatingly expressed his interest. I thought to myself, "Aharon is becoming his old self!"

One Sunday evening, a week before Rosh Hashana, we had a very exciting reunion in a Netanya restaurant with the medical teams that treated Aharon at the scene of the injury and in the helicopter. There was Dr. Itai, the physician in the helicopter; Dr. Rotem, who was on duty in Aharon's military vehicle and was wounded several days later; Ziv, the paramedic in the helicopter; and Motti, the medic who resuscitated Aharon on the ground for about forty minutes. Our hearts brimmed over with the desire to say thank you, as did the hearts of the rescuers in their desire to know us and to connect with us.

As we drove to the restaurant, I thought about the approaching reunion and the questions I wished to ask, questions whose appropriateness for a restaurant was unclear to me: What would lead someone to work tirelessly to save the life of a total stranger? What would make him feel duty-bound to do everything to save him, and then to follow up afterwards regarding his condition? Why wouldn't he leave his act of rescue behind? Had they thought about these questions? Or perhaps they had just been acting on instinct?

We met at the entrance to the restaurant. There were hugs and smiles. Even without words, the mood amongst us was sated with joy, excitement and infinite love. Not just between us but throughout the restaurant you could feel this positive, electrifying atmosphere. It was "a taste of the World-to-Come", a feeling of tangible, ideological oneness. This was no superficial posturing. Here was a pristine truth.

Dr. Itai, the physician from the Air Force's Rescue Unit 669, said that they didn't need us to say thank you. The greatest thank you, the greatest gift they could receive, was to see Aharon alive and well, talking and smiling.

Each of them told about their encounter with Aharon's injury and what they, themselves, had done. Hearing the details, you can understand why they had received citations. There was Motti the paramedic's struggle to find an air passage for Aharon via his mouth, with Aharon wounded, full of blood and having lost the normal shape of a mouth, and this after the physician's attempt on the ground to cut the wind pipe had twice failed. And all this was taking place in a crowded, narrow military vehicle, with Motti evincing amazing physical elasticity to be able to perform such a complex action. Motti understood that the situation was dire and he told the other wounded to recite psalms, because "now it's all in G-d's hands."

There was the helicopter pilot who hovered in the air for about twenty minutes and could not land due to the rockets and missiles flying every which way. In the end he understood that unless he evacuated Aharon immediately, Aharon had no chance of survival, and he decided to land despite the danger.

There was Ziv, the paramedic in the helicopter, who under conditions of darkness crouched over Aharon and had to operate, and to succeed, where the physician on the ground had twice failed. It was an operation carried out for the first time in the world in a helicopter flight under conditions of darkness. Ziv said simply, "Under operating room conditions it's a synch."

They had brought Aharon a gift. That's right! *They* brought *him* a gift. And here is what they inscribed:

"In distress you called and I rescued you" (Psalm 81:8). On January 14, 2009, our fates were intertwined. We all feel privileged to have been a part of your life, in one way or another. If only we could have met under other, happier circumstances, devoid of pain and suffering.

"We tensely followed your remarkable recovery, and none were happier than us to see, hear and to know that you had returned to us . . . The story of your life and the life of your family provides hope to many people in Israel, who draw strength and inspiration from your fortitude and determination to struggle against our enemies from within and without . . .

We salute and admire you.

Yours always,

[signatures]

At the end of the reunion, we hugged and promised to meet again.

On the Land and in the Air

We left that exciting reunion and got into the car. We were driving along when suddenly we heard on the radio about the death of Assaf Ramon in a fighter jet accident.

No!!! I cried out in a loud voice, my whole body trembling.

The son crashed on this earth and disappeared from our present world in a tragic manner, so similar to that of his father, the Israeli astronaut Ilan Ramon, of blessed memory.

Why? Why weren't they privileged to be saved and to be with us here and now? Why should things end this way for a boy who could have looked after himself and fled danger, and instead chose to give to our people? Why were we privileged to have our son Aharon here and now, whereas Assaf's mother Rona was not so privileged? Only G-d knows. The question of "why" is a cruel question that remains forever without a solution in the absence of prophets. The human mind cannot fathom such things. What, then, is left for man to do? To face the reality and to deal with it in the best, most beneficial way he can.

A father and son, buried together at Kibbutz Nahalal, one of the symbols of the renewal of Zionism and the establishment of the State of Israel. It is a place that expresses the power to make life burgeon even in a barren wilderness. Following is from an article written about Nahalal on its fifteenth birthday:

On September 11, 1921, twenty people arrived and pitched seven tents. They came without any particular plan, and without a guaranteed income source. The paltry funds granted by the United Israel Appeal were provided in dribs and drabs, and not in cash, and not when needed. Building supplies were costly, and at that time the institutions, personages and experts stood opposed to the very act of settling malignant soil with disease-infested waters and air thick with death.

The consolidation process took a long time. It involved creating something out of nothing, almost without a previous parallel. And it was accomplished amidst a tangle of mishaps and setbacks, accidents of nature, hindrance from local neighbors, the government's negative attitude, lack of means, years of drought, field mice, constant disease to man and beast, and above all else, self-doubts about building new lives amidst countless problems, social discord, mistakes, suffering, the sorrow of the individual and of the group, losses and general mourning, establishing laws and customs, rights and duties.

Yet they never lost hope. They never slackened. They toiled on and on, employing all their strength.

First came sanitation. The swamp water was run through underground clay and cement pipes to the main spring, from which, in turn, water was drawn and brought to the home gardens. Thus, the water which had previously been a breeding ground for the Anopheles mosquito which transmitted malaria, became a vehicle of blessing. True, during the first year, the sanitation work sent eighty percent of the workers to the sickbed, but life vanquished death. The water was cleansed and purified, and the place was rendered healthy. All the soil was prepared, its stones were removed and it was enhanced. Fertilizer restored to the soil its strength, the sweat of toil enriched it, and it absorbed the workers' love and devotion.

With the preparatory work, paving the road and building barns, two or three years passed, and they had not yet achieved a genuine harvest. There were not yet homes. They lived in tents, and when they finally did have a harvest, there were still mishaps aplenty. There was a shortage of beasts of burden and farm equipment; and they were smitten by drought and field mice, such that a great many years passed until a normal country farm was created.

Yet that farm was created, and it produces a varied supply of the fundamental household staples: bread, milk, vegetables, poultry and fruit. They started with cultivating field crops, trying many until they achieved respectable yields. There was the main road . . .

With graying hair, furrowed brows and wrinkled visages, they pull their plows through field and garden, watering and raking, pitchfork in hand. The goal of creating farming families engaged in a diverse enterprise, working the soil like any native of his own land, has been achieved. If you go out to see their gardens and fields, orchards and vegetable gardens, to see them packing straw, etc., you will find the various families intently devoted to their work.

Nahalal, marking fifteen years of their having settled the

homeland, together with the entire Hebrew public, can be very satisfied and proud of such stellar achievements, and may many more follow as our homeland is reborn.

Friend, how good it is to breath in the air of yesteryear! Idealism, Zionism and self-sacrifice. I remember the "Nahalal Document" publicized in 2005. People from the kibbutzim in the north came out with declaration of Zionism that looked "antiquated". Here is what appeared in the press:

> "This document is a cornerstone of the living philosophy of the Nahalal Conference and of the people of the Labor settlements," said Tzafrir Ronen, a kibbutznik from Ein Harod and the veteran of an elite army unit. Ronen said their intention was to submit the document to all the Zionist parties, so that all could adopt in as part of their platform, and "whoever does not do so will be shown to be someone who does not believe in the worldview of the classic Zionist movement which brought about the establishment of the State of Israel".
>
> "Obviously, the various shades of the Left will not understand how it is possible today to talk this way, but precisely the Labor settlements, who created the country's borders with their bodies, are the ones who can identify with those who today are fulfilling what they themselves fulfilled in the not-too-distant past," he added.

The newspapers then presented the document itself. Its first sentences follow:

> "The Land of Israel is the only historic, national home of the Jewish People, from Biblical times to the present. It was our country for a thousand years, and even when we were forcibly exiled from it, we still continued for another two thousand years to view it as our land, and a few of its children never left it. This fundamental fact led to the San Remo decision of the League of Nations from 1920, when it placed the mandate for "administering the territory of Palestine" in the hands of Britain, as "a national home for the Jewish People"."

Days of Repentance and Feasting

Days before Rosh Hashana of 2009, eight months after the injury, Aharon, Tzvia, Chaya and I arrived at the American embassy in Jerusalem to obtain visas for our trip to Arizona for surgery. We had been warned, "You mustn't make a single mistake with even one word of the forms," and those in the know had added, "They don't let you bring in cell phones."

Sure enough, when we arrived it turned out that we were missing a particular form and the clerk would not let us continue until we had filled it out precisely. It took about an hour to take care of those forms. Each of us arrived with a folder full of forms, recent pay stubs, a list of our academic institutions, you name it.

We were required to undergo a security check, twice, each time in a different room or corridor. The corridors here had double doors. We were required to give finger prints, and to pay an exorbitant service charge. We felt as though we had come before the Supreme King of Kings. It was a real preparation for the Day of Judgment.

"The Karov family to window number 3," came the announcement. It was the moment we'd been waiting for. We approached with fear and trepidation. Beyond the bullet-proof glass sat a serious looking clerk whose entire bearing expressed gravity. He turned to me and asked me two questions. I answered. He asked for Aharon's medical forms. He Xeroxed them and returned them.

"Your visas are approved and will arrive in the mail soon," he said.

I couldn't believe it. "Don't you want our pay stubs and all the documents they asked us to bring?" I asked.

"I believe you," he replied.

We left and I asked myself, "Were all the warnings for naught, or perhaps our preparations, themselves, were what made the whole thing so simple in the end? Perhaps we've got to learn from this for the Day of Judgment that is fast approaching?

The day after Rosh Hashana, our family gathered together in Jerusalem in the "Har Choma" Neighborhood for a street-naming in memory of my grandfather, Eliyahu Koren. Grandpa

Koren was born in Nuremberg, Germany, and was part of the German-Jewish Aliya to Israel during the 1930's.

One Friday, in Germany, he read a new edict in the newspaper: Any Jew wishing to leave Germany must declare all his property." That sufficed for him. Unfortunately, most of the Jews, unlike him, did not read the writing on the wall. That day, he began to organize his exodus from Germany. He and his older brother arranged their departure for Sweden, where they had business interests, and the next week they fled Germany. The older brother remained all his life in Sweden, whereas my grandfather moved to Eretz Yisrael immediately.

In Israel he became a partner in the struggle for and the rebuilding of the Land. He was the graphic artist of the Jewish National Fund. He designed the first postage stamp after the State of Israel's founding, as well as the symbol of Jerusalem. Yet first and foremost, he initiated and published the first Jewish Bible after two thousand years.

Bibles printed before then were published by Christian publishing houses. Grandpa set up teams of experts in the Hebrew language and in Biblical research. He toiled to fashion a new letter font to be used exclusively for the Bible, "the Koren font". Grandpa was a man of truth. He was not overly-impressed by outer appearances, even though he was an artist and an expert regarding aesthetics. Content and truth were enormously important to him. He toiled with precision over ever dot and tittle in order to produce something authentic. Money did not interest him, and suggestions he received to cut corners he rejected out of hand.

Before the ceremony, we went to a Jerusalem medical expert to fashion part of Aharon's missing skull. As an aside, he threw out the following words, "I think you cannot operate on the nose before you operate on the head."

We were in shock. Everything was already planned and finalized for our trip to Arizona immediately after Succot. While still in the doctor's office we called another doctor and asked his opinion. Indeed, it was very important that first you operate on the head and only then on the nose. How could it be that no one had thought about this until now? Nose doctors think about noses and head experts think about heads, and they have trouble seeing the larger picture. We understand why a person is always on the way to a destination. Here we learned once more that a person has to plan his life, but it may that reality is planning something else for him. "Many designs are in a man's mind, but it is the L-rd's plan that is accomplished" (Proverbs 19:21). I prayed and believed that this alteration would bring only goodness and blessing.

The day before Yom Kippur, Aharon called. "Dad," he said. "I'm on my way home from Mincha of Erev Yom Kippur, and I'm asking myself: Does what happened to me in the war indicate that G-d's judgment for me a year ago was not for the good?"

On the one hand, I felt happiness on hearing him say this. Aharon was returning to his spiritual and faith-based thinking. How fortunate we were to have merited that! On the other hand, however, such a question that could really throw someone off kilter.

"Look Aharon," I said, starting with an explanation that had to be kept short – the fast day was not far off. "There are three reasons for a person's suffering: (1) his own sins and shortcomings; (2) the sins and shortcomings of the community; and (3) the very fact that we live in a world that is lacking and limited, even without any sins to speak of. We have no way of knowing what caused your injury. There is no prophet to reveal that to us. A person may be suffering on behalf of the public because he is righteous. The fact that you fought on behalf of the Jewish People, and the fact that despite your mortal injury, you are recuperating, indicate that you have a lot of merits, and indicate precisely a positive judgment. From now on you've got to invest thought in the question of "How must I cope with the reality in which I live?" It is no accident that Rosh Hashana and Yom Kippur fall out at the start of the year and not at the end. Our gaze is forward."

Yom Kippur arrived. The prayers this year were like no other. We weren't just reciting the words out of the prayer book. The words burst forth from within us. "Who shall live and who shall die? Who shall come to a timely end, and who to an untimely end? Have mercy on our children and our infants!" and on and on.

Unfortunately, we become more engaged with the deeper meaning of our lives through hardship and suffering. Not in vain did Rabbi Menachem Mendel Morgensztern, the Kotzker Rebbe, say that "nothing brings perfection like a broken heart." Is it impossible for us to understand the deeper meaning of the words and to feel the reality of life's complexities without undergoing suffering?

Yom Kippur is a day that reminds us all that we are all one people. It engenders a feeling of togetherness and a generosity of spirit. We beg forgiveness and very many people pray and fast, even if they do so in their own way.

Tzvia's mother, from Kfar Giladi, related that the local garage mechanic told her, "I pray for all the wounded of Operation Cast Lead and for Aharon Karov in my own way." The media broadcast much programming about Yom Kippur, about repentance, about asking for forgiveness and about the fact that very many people find an attachment to this day, however they personalize it.

I heard an interview with the author A. B. Yehoshua, who defines himself as a heretic. He spoke about the Binding of Isaac and about his understand of its spiritual meaning. Somewhere during the interview he remarked that he was in synagogue on Rosh Hashanah and he noticed that the Binding of Isaac is mentioned throughout the service. What connection does a heretic like A.B. Yehoshua have to synagogue services on Rosh Hashanah? And yet to follow the entire service? His decisive answer to this was astonishing: "I love to hear the sound of the Shofar!"

We all know that the simplest musical instrument can produce more pleasant, polished sounds than the shofar can, and that the music produced by the shofar is neither special nor complex. So what so attracted A. B. Yehoshua, self-proclaimed heretic, into the synagogue on Rosh Hashanah? I think that perhaps that same inner voice that has attached so many Jews to the story of Aharon and to what he symbolizes also resounds within the heart of A. B. Yehoshua and beckons him to listen to the shofar blasts.

When Yom Kippur was over, Aharon and I went to meet with one of my rabbis, Rabbi Yehoshua Tzukerman, a very special Jew, and a very profound thinker as well. He has an enormous store of knowledge of all parts of the Torah and Philosophy. A broad, diverse population comes to his home and seeks out his teachings. The rabbi spoke to us about loving your fellow Jew.

"There is no greater show of one's love of Israel than army service," he said. "Religious and irreligious, Leftists and Rightists, all of them proclaim, 'We love our people, hence we are ready to fight on their behalf.' There is no difference between someone who has thought about this and is conscious of it, and someone who enlists because the law mandates it. This love is what lies at the heart of one's willingness to fight."

Afterwards Rav Tzukerman explained that being injured or – G-d forbid – dying in a war is not connected to an individual's balance sheet of merit and sin, but to the public balance sheet. Every one of us is an entire universe, yet every one of us is also only one small part of the universe. Is that a contradiction? No. The watchword is "complexity".

A week later the holiday of Succot arrived. For the past eight months, every moment of our lives had been a lesson in the meaning of the succah, the booth we go out to inhabit on Succot: Don't be tempted to think you control your life. Don't become besotted with your large, strong home. Be aware! Everything is fluid and transient in our world. Don't let this fact put you in despair. Rather, learn to live with it and to take advantage of the enormous resources hidden away in this transience.

The newspaper *Yediot Aharonot* presented an article in its holiday supplement, interviewing all seven of the citation recipients from "Cast Lead". "Heroes' Junction" was its title.

The article included points you don't hear on a daily basis:

"All seven agree on several common fundamental values: Yes, they say, it is good to die for our land, but only when there is no choice. It is better to live."

Later in the article, First Lieutenant Efraim Tehila said the following:

"When I go into battle, I am an emissary, not of my wife and daughter, but of the Jewish People."

On consideration, I think that this readiness to die for our land finds its foundation in the Binding of Isaac, which teaches us that there are things more important than one's personal life.

Captain Motti Iflach, who received a citation for saving Aharon, said, "At one point I came to the hospital to return to Aharon several items that belonged to him, and he was still under sedation . . . I wasn't sure he would survive. When you're told that someone has been in an operation for several hours, that he's got shrapnel in his brain, you wonder what sort of quality of life he's going to have. And then you get a phone call from him: 'Congratulations on the citation! I'm happy for you and I wanted to express my enormous gratitude!' When that happens, it's really exciting . . . In the phone conversation, I told him that as far as I'm concerned, the citation goes to him."

What self-sacrifice! What humility! What praise! Pure "Cast Lead"! Once more I pondered the enormous distance between the daily life of Israeli society, in which people are preoccupied with personal, mundane concerns, and special times, very specific periods, in which pure, pristine forces of idealism and unity burgeon forth, the forces of Cast Lead.

I came across Dan Margalit's book, "The Sobering". He dedicated the book to Yonatan Netanel who was killed in Cast Lead, and to the judge Aharon Barak.

During Cast Lead, Dan Margalit was in Kfar Aza, one of the towns on the edge of the Gaza Strip. He wrote:

"At the gas station before Kfar Aza I saw two female soldiers weeping over someone named Yonatan Netanel and speaking effusively in his praise. They were standing in the crowded cafeteria, weeping bitterly and talking non-stop about an officer who had worn a knitted yarmulka. About two days later I felt a sort of compulsion to console specifically that soldier's family who were mourning in Jerusalem. My conversation with Yonatan's parents and friends is preserved in my heart as a dialogue that could not be heard in any other sector of Israeli society, and it is for that reason that the book is dedicated to his memory."

What really prodded Margalit to go to the Netanel home? What about the female soldier's words caught his attention and touched his heart?

I think that those words, that "could not be heard in any other sector" are very certainly heard in all the sectors, albeit in a voice so still that the ear can barely hear them. When those words are voiced loud and clear, the still voice, that was already inside you, encounters the loud voice and bonds with it. It bonds with it, and it rushes to the Netanel home, which expresses the voice of purity and unity loud and clear.

Hoshana Rabba Night arrived, a night on which for generations Jews have learned Torah until morning. I taught a Torah lecture in Ra'anana. The topic was, "Even if a sharp sword is pressed against one's neck, one should not despair." After the lecture, a Jew approached me and told me that he had been wounded in the First Lebanon War. He related:

"After your son was injured, I was in the *"Beit HaLochem"* rehabilitation center for disabled veterans. Several wounded soldiers told me: 'Let's see how that father talks after they put Aharon through several medical board sessions. For sure he will be bitter after that, and he won't broadcast such faith any more.' Every time we meet, I remind them of their pessimistic forecast."

Sure enough, dealing with the Defense Ministry is a recipe for difficulties and testy words. I, too, think some changes have to be made in the way they run things.

Yet you've got to see the whole picture, Aharon's miracle and the things the Defense Ministry does indeed help out with, and they are many. The Defense Ministry accompanies us and helps a lot with surgical operations, treatment and with our many needs. Even if one day I try to effect changes in the array of relations between Israel's wounded soldiers and the Defense Ministry, it will not be coming from a place of bitterness and confrontation, but out of a genuine effort to improve things, out of a sense of gratitude.

Almost nine months after the injury, my wife and I stopped at a toy store to buy a gift for our granddaughter on her second birthday. At the store entrance stood a guard examining with his eyes those coming and going. "You're from T.V.," he said. "How is your son?" he asked, with the heavy accent of a Russian immigrant. Nine months later, the story was still engraved in the hearts of much of the Jewish People.

Part V | Get Well Quick

Operation "Engine Cover"

That was that. At last the schedule for the operations had been decided upon.

But just a moment. This was the second time these decisions had been made. Would the schedule actually play out this time? Only G-d knew. "First you've got to operate on the head and only then on the nose," one of the experts had ruled.

So the head operation would be first, on January 2, 2009, and the first reconstructive nose operation would take place on February 22 in Arizona. The second date was likewise Aharon and Tzvia's first wedding anniversary.

Aharon's brother-in-law called the approaching head operation "Operation Engine Cover". A large segment of Aharon's skull had become infected and had been removed, and now a replacement was needed. Until now, Aharon had been going around missing part of his skull, and he had to be very careful to avoid blows to that area, which could have directly harmed his brain. Whenever Aharon scratched the left side of his head, I would say to him, "Be careful. You are scratching your brain."

The missing piece of skull was noticeable, and whoever saw him would be astonished or alarmed. I can't remember to this day ever seeing someone walking down the street with such a head indentation. In general, such people are found in hospitals. Yet with Aharon, everything moved at a different pace. Sure enough, on Succot Aharon went with Tzvia and her brothers on a hiking trip to the Ein Gedi area.

For two days, Aharon hiked like someone who is healthy in every way. He chose a four-hour hiking path for good walkers and drove a jeep on a challenging jeep route. For our part, we, his parents, encouraged and prodded him to be careful and to slow down his pace, but we also knew that this was his strong point, confronting difficulties and viewing himself as healthy in every way. Despite the problems and despite the headaches, as far as he was concerned, "everything was perfect".

What do you do when your skull bone is missing? You prepare a replacement, made of special, plastic material. You take external measurements, and you also do a computer simulation of what the head is missing in order to prepare a replacement that will be compatible with the missing shape. On the one hand, it sounded like science fiction. On the other hand, we felt like they were talking about a sort of carpentry work.

Two physicians would collaborate in this operation – a brain surgeon, Dr. Jackson, knew Aharon's head and brain very well from the inside, and Professor Sela, an expert in reconstructing skulls and in creating replacements. The operation is not simple. Altogether, opening up the skull requires us to pray a lot that it should succeed and that there should be no mishaps or infections.

Precisely nine months after the injury, Aharon and Tzvia arrived at our home at 10:30 PM. Occasionally the two of them visit, but this time the visit was unexpected. The twinkle in Aharon's eyes said something, but I didn't understand and I didn't guess. We talked, catching up on things and just chatting. They brought us a disk on which had been filmed a reenactment of the incident in which Aharon had been injured. The reenactment had been made by Aharon's company commander, Ro'i. He executed the reenactment, recounting for half-an-hour about the mission they had been on, about the explosion and the rescue. The disk added to what we knew – following the explosion, most of Aharon's body had been buried under the ruins of the roof and the entire second floor that had collapsed from the powerful intensity of the explosion. His personal weapon and some of his other personal effects had been buried deep under the ruins of the home and only with heavy machinery could it have been extracted. Obviously, they did not do that. Aharon was not breathing and did not react, and only when he was forcibly pulled out of the ruins did he show signs of life by snorting. "The fact that Aharon's head was not buried under the ruins like the rest of his body was a great miracle," said Ro'i, the company commander, on the disk.

Suddenly Aharon said, "We wanted to tell you that there is something in Tzvia's womb." Every announcement of this sort from our children is very exciting. Look! Our children are becoming parents! Look! Another pure soul will appear in the world. Look! Once more we are going to have a grandchild!

All the same, this time that excitement was one of a kind. Our hearts soared to the heavens, seeking to reach the Throne of Glory, and to say, "Thank you!" Aharon and Tzvia's ability to bring life into the world was another part of the great miracle we had merited.

Once again G-d had revived the dead. Aharon was alive in the truest sense. He was privileged to bring new life into the world. I felt as though we had been through nine renewed months of conception with Aharon, and here we were, starting the nine months of conception of his son or daughter. I felt as though the expression "revival of the dead" was a bit modest for what we were undergoing.

My cell phone rang. It was Tova from the United Israel Appeal. She said, "We are having a fund-raising evening for the State of Israel, a major event in Rome. Would you and Aharon be prepared to come to Rome for that evening?"

"Is it important that we come?" I asked. "Is it worth your flying us in for one evening?" Tova explained to me that all the organizers felt that Aharon's story melts hearts and thus opens wallets. I asked about the date of the event and it turned out that it was right before Aharon's surgery. We would be on the way to Arizona, not Rome.

A day later, Tova called again. "We would like very much to film Aharon and you with Ziv the paramedic who received a citation for his rescue. That film clip will itself move the hearts of Rome's Jews." Apparently, most of world Jewry are unimpressed by three twelfth graders running around the Diaspora slandering the Jewish State and the I.D.F. Neither are they influenced by the anti-Semitic Goldstone report.

On Monday, Ziv and his wife and the film crew arrived at our home in Karnei Shomron. The meeting was pleasant and exciting. Aharon and Ziv sat in chairs on the lawn in our backyard and we had to remain inside in order not to disturb the filming.

"After having been mortally wounded, how do you relate today to the country and to the army?" the director asked Aharon. My wife and I listened tensely from the doorway. Aharon replied, "I want to continue contributing to the country. If I can, I will contribute to the army, and if not, I will contribute in some other way."

A week later they called from the Libi Fund to ask if we'd be willing to participate in an evening on behalf of Libi France.

That evening I gave a lecture in a Jerusalem community center. At the entranceway to the center, a woman in her forties approached me and asked to speak to me. "This may sound bizarre to you," she began, and I thought to myself, "We've been through a lot of bizarre things during recent months" . . .

"I am an alternative medicine practitioner," she went on, presenting her business card, "and the day that Aharon was injured and it was announced on T.V., I immediately began treating Aharon long-distance. I treated him for an hour-and-a-half. I think I can help him and I would like to perform several treatments on him." I just didn't know what to think or what to say. One thing was clear. "So many practitioners had tried to help Aharon in so many ways, and probably they all had a share in his recovery. And even if there was no medical benefit to be had from it, the fact that many people prayed and devoted their time to Aharon's recovery had an effect in Heaven.

The next day, my cell phone rang.

"Hello, this is a newswoman from the Hareidi newspaper *"Bamishpacha"*. I was at your lecture yesterday at the community center in Jerusalem, and I would like to write an article about the things you said." She went on, "I thought the newspaper's editor would say that Aharon's story had been overdone already. Yet when I suggested the idea to him, he was really happy to do an article about your talk." She added that Aharon's story spoke to people and was relevant for people even now, months after the injury. Two days later I received the article by email. It turned out she had written two articles. One was a summary of the story of his recovery, and the other was a summary of my lecture as far as the ethical question of the "groom going off to war".

It turns out that even the Hareidi public, which seems to be far removed from the army and to have a negative attitude to the State, understands and longs for the atmosphere of giving that exists in the army. I recall that the first time I walked in the Meah She'arim neighborhood after Aharon's injury, quite a number of Hareidim ran after me and said excitedly, "You're the father of that officer, right? How is he?" ending off with the phrase, "I salute you both!"

I was surprised by how they identified me and the respect they held for an officer in the army. There you are! There are things that peal away the external trappings of our lives.

Almost a Year

About two months before the first anniversary of Cast Lead, the media began to bombard us with requests for anniversary interviews with Aharon and Tzvia. The couple decided to take part in a feature article for the newspaper *Yedi'ot Aharonot*, and to have just Aharon be interviewed for the Channel 2 Television station.

The question of exposure versus the desire to remain anonymous remained a constant point of discussion for us after the injury. The first month, we were totally preoccupied with Aharon. After that, however, when Aharon's recuperation process proceeded positively and went into high gear, we had little strength to deal with that question as well. In actual fact, however, this was the first time Aharon was being interviewed by the media, and obviously, it was also Tzvia's first time, besides the first day of the injury, in which she expressed words of strength and valor to the media.

As the anniversary approached, as part of the discussions about interviews, which obviously brought up memories from the year that had passed, I decided to review all the pictures and film clips we had taken since the injury. More precisely, one of our sons had taken charge of that task out of his love for photography. I was excited and astonished to be looking back. There were the very difficult sights from the beginning. Also the event, remembered as one of great joy, Aharon's first steps now looked sadder than they had then. Aharon's face, so morose, his lackluster eyes, bulging out of their sockets, his gait, like that of a drunkard teetering hither and thither . . . everything looked more somber.

But back then, in those days, we felt immense joy. We saw the progress and the great miracle – Aharon walking – and we paid no heed to the small details. One more I thought about the great good fortune that during such incidents we are not free for cold, rational thinking. Rather, we flow with the reality. It was all from G-d.

For the first time I was seeing the Chassidic singer Avraham Fried standing by Aharon's bed, quietly singing a soulful tune. Aharon was not yet with us. He had not yet awoken. His head was bandaged, and he was not moving a single limb. Machines and tubes were connected to his head and to other parts of his body. Avraham Fried was emotional, and he slowly approached the bed that Aharon was lying on without movement. He hummed the Chabad wedding tune. I was seeing all this for the first time – when Avraham Fried arrived at the hospital, I was having one of the few hours of sleep that I had during those days – and I shuddered.

I asked myself: "From where did we draw the strength to deal with such a terrible situation during those long hours and days?" and I thanked the Creator for the strength He had granted us to look towards the future, to believe that things would turn out well and to ignore the situation.

To no less a degree, I was thankful for the resources He had given us to deal with the new routine in our lives. It was a routine that contained within it a lot of good and progress, but which also contained quite a number of difficulties and unexpected things to deal with.

Inside the Head

Five days before Aharon's surgery on his head, I was in the Huga Water Park with all the students of the yeshiva. The twelfth grade had prepared water activities for all the students, and at the end of the day, they joined together to pray for Israel's drought to end. My cell phone rang and I could see that it was Dr. Jackson, the surgeon who would be performing the operation.

Truth be told, I was tense with worry. Why should he want to talk to me?

"I would like to ask a favor of you," he began. I calmed down. "In another week-and-a-half, dozens of physicians will be arriving from the United States and they would like to hear Aharon's story. I would like several of the pictures that you took."

A perfectly understandable request.

"And I would also like the article you wrote before his injury on the topic, 'A Newlywed Goes Off to War'." This, by contrast, was not so easy to understand. What need was there for an article of that sort at a medical conference?

"I would like to convey to them as well, your spirit and worldview." I had heard many times already since Aharon's injury about the spirit and worldview broadcast by the family. Over and over I could sense just how much that spirit had touched much of the Jewish People.

Sunday, the day before the operation, Aharon checked in to Tel HaShomer Hospital. We asked for a private room. The head nurse told us that there was such a room, but that there was a problem. "The room's number is thirteen, and the question is whether or not you want such a room."

My wife asked, "What is the problem?"

"Thirteen is bad luck", replied the nurse.

"Quite the contrary," said my wife. "It's a good number."

"Really?" asked the nurse.

True, amongst the nations there is a superstition that the number thirteen brings bad luck. The source of this belief is not known, but it is very ancient and known throughout the world.

There are buildings in which after the twelfth floor you immediately come to the fourteenth floor.

In Judaism, by contrast, thirteen is a good, blessed number. At age thirteen, a male undertakes mitzvah observance, G-d is know for His thirteen merciful traits, and thirteen is the numerical value of both the Hebrew words אהבה-*ahava*, "love", and אחד-*echad*, "one". Rambam concluded that the number of principles of Jewish faith is thirteen.

The nurse was astonished to hear this. "What a pity," I thought to myself, "that so many Jews know and believe in Christian superstitions and but do not know the beliefs of Judaism."

As the operation neared, our hearts filled with prayers and hopes that this should be the last operation on Aharon's skull. It became clear to us that a plastic surgeon would be participating in the operation to help with the stitches afterwards. The skin on Aharon's head had become thin and delicate from previous operations, and one had to know how to sew in the stitches so that in the future the stitches would not open and the skin would not be torn.

Monday Morning, at 6:45, they came to take Aharon to the operating room. We accompanied him with loud words of encouragement and silent prayers.

Tzvia said to me, "You wouldn't believe what happened yesterday." I tensed up. "We were in the mall by the hospital and a mother and her daughter approached us. The mother asked, "You're Aharon, right?" Aharon, with a mischievous smile, answered, "No I'm not! What gave you that idea?" The mother and daughter were perplexed. I hurried to make things right and to say that he really was Aharon. Right then, the daughter, over twenty years old, began to weep and couldn't stop. Her mother said, "She wants to salute you and she is overwrought." Tzvia added, "Ten months later, people still weep and get excited."

Ten months had passed and the public's attachment to Aharon had not lessened one iota. I felt this in the hospital every moment. Doctors, nurses, patients and guests would stop us, bless us, offer us encouragement and salute us. One man, who introduced himself as the manager of the "Aroma" Cafe, shook my hand and told us that he had been following us since the injury. "I salute you!" A young boy stopped and said, "You're the father of . . . Right?" Some people just turned their gaze towards us, and their eyes spoke volumes.

We descended by elevator to the operating rooms. In the elevator stood a man whose two arms were made of iron. He had no hands and no fingers. He smiled to Aharon and said, "Good luck!"

We entered the operation prep room. Another five people were waiting to enter the operating rooms. All of them, without exception, looked at Aharon with a look of identification, and some said, "Hats off to you!" and "Good luck!"

At 8:30 AM the operation began. Every one of us, each in his own way, turned inward, whether in prayer, Torah learning, rumination or internal dialogue. We were all praying that this should be the last operation on Aharon's brain or skull.

During this time we received many text messages: "Get better quick" . . . "Our fingers are crossed" . . . and many more.

At about 11:30 AM Dr. Jackson and Professor Sela emerged from the operating theater. They said that the skull replacement implantation had been successful, but they cautiously asked a question. From the question and the look on their faces, it became clear that at the end of the operation, a mini-drama had taken place around Aharon.

At the end of the operation they had tried to wake up Aharon a bit to see if he was moving his limbs, and to check if there was any damage to his functioning. A skull operation of this sort can damage all sorts of functioning. The physicians detected that his right hand was weaker than his left. They were anxious over the possibility that they had inadvertently caused some damage. They considered quickly taking him for a CT, but in the end it was decided that they would give Aharon more time to awaken, and then they would examine him again. They delicately informed us that they saw that his right hand was weaker than his left. We breathed a sigh of relief, saying to ourselves, "So that's the whole story . . ." and we explained to them that indeed, the injury to his brain had made his right hand weaker than his left, and that at Tel HaShomer Hospital, in the Rehabilitation Department, they were toiling to improve his right hand. We could immediately see that a stone had been lifted from their hearts.

Once more it had been proven that the reality visible to the naked eye is deceiving. Aharon's left hand had absorbed a direct blow and hundreds of shrapnel pieces were embedded in it. That hand, which had had its circulation cut off for over and hour with a tourniquet, and which the doctors had fought to save, had totally normal functioning. By contrast the right hand, which from the outside looked flawless, and hadn't even been scratched, had difficulty functioning due to the injury to the brain.

Aharon began to recover and to come back to himself. He lay in a bed in the Neuro-surgical Department. His friend Yisrael called. Aharon couldn't yet answer the phone. I answered and Yisrael asked how Aharon was doing. "Thank G-d", I replied. Aharon heard and he asked who I was talking to, and he said to me testily, "Tell him, 'Thank G-d, excellent.'" Aharon was still groggy and in pain, but that's how he is, to insist on saying, "Excellent".

By nightfall, we had been through several unpleasant episodes with Aharon. Yet the next morning, Aharon was as good as new. Ever smiley and active, he did everything himself and spoke about going home. Professor Singer, head of Intensive Care, came to visit and said, "Look, I talked to Aharon. It's just marvelous. He looks great."

Dr. Jackson wanted Aharon to leave the hospital as fast as possible. A hospital is a place to get better, but it's also a place to contract illnesses.

Three days after the operation, Aharon was sent home.

Now then, we still had a long way to go to resume normal life, but the worst was behind us. As long as his brain had been exposed, without protection, there was a great fear of his getting hit in the head, and this prevented Aharon from doing many things. Aharon felt that this operation would restore his freedom and a return to routine. Only a small part of his head remained without a skull and without a replacement. It was explained to us to that there was a problem with going near the left ear, lest Aharon not be able to open his mouth. We would wait for some future medical invention to close that opening as well.

Operation "Engine Cover" was over.

Several days after the operation, Aharon showed me that his right hand, which, as noted, had suffered from weakness due to the injury to his brain, had now returned to almost normal functioning apart from the index finger, which refused to bend. "The Rehab physician told me that very often after such an operation, the pressure on the brain is lessened and the situation improves," Aharon explained.

Not long after, Aharon called: "Dad, please check for me when the firing range is open on Fridays in Karnei Shomron."

I was a bit in shock. "What's going on?" I asked, and he replied, "I've got to renew my pistol license."

I checked it for him and called him back. "Tell me," I asked. "Just how do you intend to shoot? The index finger of your right hand, which is supposed to pull the trigger, doesn't work!" I figured Aharon hadn't thought about that problem.

"Oh, I forgot to tell you," he said. "Several days ago the finger returned to normal functioning. Things don't fall out of my hand anymore." I was silent. What can you possibly say when gradually, step by step, your son is returning to normal?

Friday Afternoon I called Aharon to hear about the firing range.

"Actually, I didn't do so bad," he said.

Who is mighty?

Friday Night, ten months after the injury, I went to a festive "*Shalom Zachar*" at the home of friends. My friend, already mentioned above, was mortally wounded at the Hamezah Outpost during the Yom Kippur War, and was saved by a great miracle. Years later, he once more had one foot in the grave, but he returned to us. Thursday Night, his first grandson was born. It's customary that on the first Friday Night after the birth, families make a "*Shalom Zachar*" celebration to thank G-d and to pray for the welfare [*shalom*] of the new male [*zachar*] infant.

An infant is born into a non-perfect world, and Shabbat turns our attention to the better, loftier aspects of life. My friend spoke of his great excitement over the appearance of new life in the world, after he, himself, had several times experienced a sort of rebirth, and his great joy on being privileged to become a grandfather.

Suddenly a resident of our town, Professor Shimon Reif, approached me and said, "I've got a relative in England who had a bad stroke six years ago. Since then, he has been paralyzed and found it difficult to talk. I called him before Shabbat to ask him how he was, and he asked me, 'How is Aharon Yehoshua doing?' I didn't understand who he was referring to. He then repeated, 'How is Aharon Yehoshua, the wounded soldier, doing?' I asked him if he was referring to Aharon Karov, and he said, 'Since his injury, I have been praying for his recovery every day.'"

I thought to myself, "What heroism! A paralyzed man, living in England, finds the strength to remember a soldier he doesn't know and to pray for him daily. He even finds the strength to ask how he is despite his own difficulties speaking." And ten months after the injury, he was still praying for him, and he remembered his name and was worried about him.

When eleven months had passed since the injury, I realized that for a long time I had been thinking about the way people relate to Aharon as a hero. Everywhere we went, we would hear the words, "brave hero". I found this very strange. Had people pitied him and related to him as an unfortunate, that I would understand. But a hero? Nothing at all had been said in the media about his activities in the war. It had not been pointed out that he bravely charged terrorists, and nothing had been said about his physical and mental prowess. All that the public knew was that Aharon had gone off to war the day after his wedding, and that he had been mortally wounded.

So why a hero?

Did nobody understand what they were saying?

The family, of course, recognized his enormous valor. His ability to cope with the injury, with the pain and the changes in his life's plans, astounded us anew almost every day. The constant smile on his face even when he was in pain, his assertion that 'things weren't so bad," taught us a chapter in courage. Yet surely the public was unaware of all this. So why did they relate to him as a hero?

As Chanuka was approaching, almost a year after the military operation, I was swamped with requests to give talks about valor. It seemed very obvious to all the people asking that Chanuka and valor belong to Aharon Karov. I talked about the fact that despite the conventional thinking that links valor to activism and charging into battle, our sages teach that the foundation of valor is restraint, self-control. "Who is mighty? He who conquers his passions." Valor means self-restraint and conquering our egoistical leanings. It means the ability to control our strong, basic proclivity for thinking only about ourselves, and the ability to give free reign to our deep-set, pristine desire to help out, to assist and to grant life to others.

All the heroism of the soldier charging the enemy in battle begins with the valor of self -restraint, in which the soldier places aside his personal fear and his anxieties about what is going to happen to him and to his personal life. Every soldier who enters battle cries out, "I am foregoing my personal life for the sake of the nation and the country." Even if no one else hears this cry, and even if the soldier, himself, does not hear the cry, and is unaware of its meaning, the cry still resonates on its own.

I also gave this talk to the officers of the Paratroopers' Brigade. One of the senior officers asked, "Why is this valor, which vanquishes egotism, only revealed rarely, in difficult circumstances? Will that change in the future?"

I spoke of optimism in life, about having faith in our people and about the challenge facing every one of us to bring this life force to constant fulfillment.

I think Aharon's story captivated the entire public due to his being "a groom who set out for battle from his wedding celebration". The story gave full expression to the rejection of one's personal life in favor of the public welfare, and it linked up with the increasing public loathing for the egotism permeating society. It turns out that everyone is weary of shallow lives in which the individual stands at center. Everyone longs for a different type of life, for a more public-spirited existence in which people think about their fellow man and feel "responsible for one another" (*Shavuot* 39a).

That evening, following my lecture to the Paratroopers, a female officer who had been in touch with us since Aharon's injury called me. She said that the lecture had been good, but that for her, something had been missing.

"What was missing?" I asked, and she answered without hesitation, "I know that Aharon's condition was hopeless. I was waiting to hear from where you derived the strength of your faith and spirit. How did you remain optimistic, and how did you cope with the difficulties? I wanted to explore that coping process in depth."

She had asked, so I said, "We'll have to find another time to elucidate your question."

G-d gave every one of us strengths. The question is, to what degree and by what means does each individual toil to connect his practical life to the spiritual forces within him.

Several days before, Tzvia and Aharon had surprised us by agreeing to be interviewed by the newspaper *Yediot Aharonot*. Since the injury, it had been very hard for Tzvia to deal with public exposure. Yet thanks to our unending encounter with the broader public, we understood that such exposure can strengthen a lot of people. The closer we got to the anniversary of Operation Cast Lead, the more the media's pressure to interview us increased.

As the interview came nearer, Tzvia read us a section from a diary she had kept over recent months. She wrote that she drew strength from Aharon's valor. When she saw how Aharon fought for his life, how he accepted his situation and how he coped with his pains, she drew strength to cope as well.

Without a doubt, Tzvia is a great hero as far as all the things she is coping with. A bride, forced to be separated on her wedding day from her new husband who went off to fight on behalf of the Jewish People, and compelled after a week-and-a-half to deal with a husband who is mortally wounded, needs infinite strength and valor. We bless our good fortune that we and Aharon have been privileged to have such a bride.

Starting the Wednesday before the article's publication in *Yediot Aharonot*, the newspaper began advertising in the media that the article was going to appear. Thursday Morning, Page 1 of *Yediot Aharonot* was emblazoned with pictures of Aharon and Tzvia with the astounding scenery of the Samarian Mountains in the background. The headline cried out "Exclusive"! The quotation the newspaper chose to use was from Aharon, "I told my wife, 'Even if I've got no nose and no skull, we are happy." What a sentence! What valor and what a positive view of life! In the article, Aharon said, "Since the injury, I am so happy." How is it possible to understand his words? Can someone severely injured be happy? Such is the valor of accepting G-d's justice and accepting reality. Our job is to live and to cope with that reality positively. To acknowledge what we've got. Such is Aharon's valor – accepting G-d's justice happily.

On Friday, a massive article appeared. I read with astonishment:

"Just eleven months have passed, and the couple looking at their wedding pictures is very different from the couple that was photographed in them. These are Tzvia, twenty-two, her head covered with a kerchief, and Aharon, on his way to a series of complex operations with a plastic surgeon in the United States. Aharon was the most severely wounded soldier of Cast Lead. Only now is his face once more starting to remind one of the handsome young man smiling in the pictures, but with the look in his eyes he smiles and radiates joy even greater than that of the groom on his wedding day. He has the look of someone who has seen death, but whose life has been returned to him . . .

"Here is what Tzvia wrote in her diary on January 16, 2009: 'Two days have already passed since the injury. Two days in a hospital, two days in which my heroic husband is fighting for his life, persevering, waging a true battle, a battle for his life. It is simply amazing to see my husband's tremendous resources, his enormous fortitude that surprises all the doctors and everyone else . . . Darling, I want you to know that you give me strength. Can you believe it? You, in your condition, give me strength. I promise. Every reaction, every sign of life, shows me what enormous resources you have . . .'"

"The main reason we had any interest at all in talking now is the Jewish People. It is impossible to describe how many people came and worried and prayed for him. Starting the first day, they inundated Intensive Care. I truly believe that the prayers were what helped most – with everyone united in their prayers and concern. This is also our opportunity to say thank you."

That Friday I got a call from Avner, who was my commander in my special Reserves unit for about twelve years. He was the commander who during army drills would prod us forward with the saying, "When we finish, you can go," by which he meant that when we finished the drill we would be walking another fifteen kilometers. I could hear the excitement in his voice. "I read Aharon's article and I just wept and wept." We heard about a lot of tears flowing after the article. Tears of identification, tears of emotion and tears of joy.

Dr. Yossi Villian of Haifa called and told us, "I wrote a poem on the inspiration of your son's story, and it was put to music. If you want to hear it, go into YouTube and listen."

Sunday Evening a feature story was broadcast about Aharon on Channel Two News. Their Internet news site wrote, "Aharon Karov has been named the most seriously wounded soldier of Cast Lead. Here he tells about his rehabilitation, which has been classed a medical miracle . . . He transmits a message of faith and hope, thanks everyone who helped him and offers encouragement to the wounded. Watch this hero's exciting interview."

Amongst other things, Aharon was photographed in the report with the street sign where we live in the background: "The Hope". The interviewer perhaps asked and perhaps declared that Aharon's having grown up on "Hope Street" had a role in shaping his great, characteristic optimism.

The phone didn't stop ringing: "We saw the feature and we were in tears" [and so were we]. . . . "I'm organizing a musical event to be held in the Nokia Stadium and we'd like to invite him to the performance" . . . "I'd like to give Aharon a gift. I won't harass him. I'll just give it to him and leave." There was no end to the phone calls and surprises. A dear man from Hadera arrived to give Aharon a gift and to look at him "for two minutes and no more." One of my sons showed me that on Facebook someone had opened an Aharon Karov Facebook page, with about four thousand responses saluting Aharon and expressing identification with him and Tzvia.

Yet one of the most exciting of them all was the following phone call:

"Hi, this is Tal, sister of the late Benny. We saw the features and we are excited and happy for you."

As you may recall, Benny was the Reserves soldier who was brought in to Beilinson Intensive Care during the early days of Aharon's injury. He had been mortally wounded in a traffic accident and he passed away after several days. Our lives were bound up with theirs, even if that had found no practical fulfillment. A key chain with a photo of Benny is on me constantly. And here they had found the strength to call and to share in our joy and in the general excitement of the Israeli public.

I thought with satisfaction: "My people are made of cast lead. You've just got to pull the right switch to reveal that."

Preparations for "Operation 'Nose Reconstruction'"

Sunday at 11:00 PM, the phone rang, and on the other side was Avishai of *Ezra LaMarpei*. "Rav Firer conveys that Dr. Menick of Arizona has landed in Israel and tomorrow at 10:00 AM he will see you at Tel HaShomer." I was surprised and excited. We wanted so much to have the opportunity to meet the doctor, for him to see Aharon, before we arrived in Arizona. Who knew if what he had seen in the pictures would jibe with what he would see for real? We wanted to meet the man who would be operating on Aharon.

We arrived at Tel HaShomer at 10:00 AM and we were told to wait. We understood that the doctor had just that moment finished an operation and that he was going to be lecturing to plastic surgeons who had convened at the hospital. "Karov, come inside," called to us the deputy head of Plastic Surgery at Tel HaShomer.

We entered a room in which there were about another six senior physicians. Dr. Menick showed himself to be a man of pleasant demeanor, calm and full of patience, both with us and with the physicians asking questions. He examined Aharon and lectured to them all about his plans for reconstructing his nose. "I will remove skin and tissue from his forehead and move some from the left side to the right side, and . . ." I felt like I was in a lecture on car repairs. I asked questions that troubled us, about the operations and about Aharon's ability to have free movement afterwards. The answers were given clearly and patiently. "I believe we will achieve results that will satisfy you," he concluded.

We were about to celebrate Chanuka, the holiday symbolizing the victory of spirit over matter. The Macabees' spiritual valor was the decisive factor that brought about their victory, much more so than their physical might. In another week we would be flying to Arizona. Our preparations entered high gear. Our cell phones were being inundated with text messages and phone calls. Blessings and encouragement for the departure being forced on us were coming in from army commanders, public figures, media personalities and, obviously, family and friends.

For example, Sivan Rahav-Meir, who had interviewed Aharon for Channel 2 about two weeks before, wrote, "You should be about to go to the U.S. Good luck and get well quick. And thanks once more for giving me the privilege of exciting and strengthening hundreds of thousands of people."

Calls from Jews in the U.S. likewise grew more and more plentiful, like the oil of the Chanuka miracle. We received a call from Bat-Sheva of Tucson, whose husband is a physician and a medical lecturer at the University of Arizona, and she said, "I am at your service. Whatever you want or need, call me," and she gave me her phone number.

A fifteen-hour flight is no simple matter for anyone, all the more so for Aharon, who had suffered an injury to his brain, and it was hard to know how he would make out with the flight. The Defense Ministry attached a paramedic to us to accompany us on the flight. He called and said, "Hi, this is Yair from Ofra. I am the paramedic who will be accompanying you." His voice broadcast confidence and calm. From our conversation it became clear that Yair had both medical expertise and experience. He gave his all to ensure that we benefited from that.

We set out for the Airport.

The flight to Los Angeles, as noted, lasted about fifteen hours, a long time to spend in the air. The feeling of hanging in the air was reminiscent of the first weeks after the injury. Then, as well, I felt like I was hanging between heaven and earth. This time, however, we were literally in midair, much simpler than when the "lack of solid ground under our feet" constituted a psychological sensation.

Fifteen hours of nighttime. A bizarre darkness. We took off in the nighttime of Eretz Yisrael and we continued on into the nighttime of the United States. The holiday of Chanuka lit up the night, and the fact that we had reached the point of dealing with the aesthetic repercussions of Aharon's injury lit up the darkness and exile into which we were headed.

I pondered whether it was any coincidence that we ended up in the Diaspora for the operation precisely on Chanuka. Surely the Macabees' having taken responsibility and having benefited from miracles was very similar to our own case.

Seated in front of us were two women becoming acquainted. It was hard not to hear their conversation. Both were Israelis who had left Israel, the spiritual pinnacle of life, to live in America. Both were returning to their homes in Los Angeles after visiting their sons in Israel. As for the sons, one has just been inducted and the other was about to be discharged. It was clear to them and to their sons that despite their living in a foreign land, they would serve in the Israel Defense Forces. "This is not obvious to all the Israelis in our community," said the one to the other.

During the flight, one of the stewards approached Aharon and Tzvia and announced, "The pilot invites you into the cockpit." Aharon and Tzvia were surprised but agreed happily. For a quarter-of-an-hour, the pilot explained to them about the flight and about the jet. Obviously, pictures were also taken in the cockpit. After some time, a stewardess brought Aharon a gift on behalf of the flight crew.

In the Los Angeles Airport Rabbi David Toledano was waiting for us. We did not know him. He had called my office the previous week and asked how he could be of assistance. He said, "This is Toledano from Los Angeles. I read the story in *Yediot Aharonot.* I understand you will be arriving in the U.S. next week, and I very much want to help."

I explained to him that we would be landing in Los Angeles and waiting there several hours for the flight to Tucson. I asked his assistance in finding a kosher restaurant where we could eat breakfast, because I knew that on the flight to Tucson, there would be no kosher food. "You've got nothing to worry about. I will come to the airport and take you to a first class restaurant, and on a short tour of Los Angeles."

And he really did provide first-class service. It was morning in Los Angeles. Everyone was racing to work, and David Toledano was totally free for us, as though he had been born just for that. First he took us to a synagogue so we could recite the morning prayers of the fourth day of Chanuka. There, a surprise awaited us. Besides a sumptuous breakfast, about ten Jews had gathered there to meet us, including the head of the Los Angeles community of Sephardic Jews from Allepo, Syria and the mayor of Beverly Hills, Jimmy Delshad, who is Jewish. "I told Jimmy you were coming and he said he was putting all else aside to meet you," said Rabbi Toledano.

"The mayor of the wealthiest city in the United States freed up two hours of his time to meet simple Jews from Eretz Yisrael!?" I wondered with excitement. After the emotional meeting, we toured Beverly Hills and the city of entertainment and imagination. Then we flew to Tucson. At the airport, before boarding the plane, a young girl approached Aharon and said to him, "I salute you." That's right, even on alien soil they remember and identify Aharon.

At the Tucson airport they were waiting for us, as well. Bat Sheva from the Jewish Community of Tucson was there to pick us up. "I am at your service," she proclaimed, and as we found out, she meant every word of this. Over the next three weeks, she would be available for us whenever we liked.

As I have already said, and not cynically, "Every Jew is responsible for every other."

The Tucson Exile

Tucson, Arizona is not a large city by American standards. It has about a million inhabitants. It is a desert town reminiscent of the towns in the old Wild West movies, aside from the fact that the roads are paved. The weather is like the winter in Israel. It's hot during the day and cool in the evening. During the summer, the temperatures reach 48 Celsius.

We were there during the Christmas season. Every window and street corner evinced signs of the holiday. They were celebrating the birth of the man in whose name the Jews' cruelest persecutors acted. In the name of their religion, they murdered many millions of Jews and many many more people who were not Jewish.

About thirty thousand Jews live in Tucson. Wherever we went, Jews approached us, blessed us on our arrival and wished us a speedy recovery. In one home we saw lights in the shape of a Jewish star on one side, and signs of Christianity on the other. Apparently, that was one more person who felt torn.

There are two Orthodox synagogues in Tucson. Both face a daily battle to attain the required quorum of ten worshippers. Once the synagogue has nine worshippers in place, the sextant begins calling a list of potential participants and asking them to come and complete the quorum.

The Jews of Tucson are fine people, but they have been confused by the Exile. With thirty thousand Jews, it is very hard to find twenty men to maintain daily services. Certainly more than that number are praying privately. Presumably more than twenty Jews light Chanuka candles. Yet the reality is very sad and painful. The material reality of daily life is overwhelming. Whoever is entirely caught up with material survival and does not free himself nor set aside time for his spiritual world, is lost. Such a person would be lost anywhere, but especially in the exile. By contrast, Eretz Yisrael, the Jewish State, conducts part of its life according to Judaism – the Sabbath, the Jewish holidays and Yom Kippur are days of rest and abstinence from work. These days instill, consciously or unconsciously, something of the spirituality of the Jewish People into its inhabitants.

It is no coincidence that throughout the United States, the assimilation rate is about seventy percent, and obviously, that is so not only in the United States, but in all the diasporas. Jews there face an almost impossible trial. If one does not devote a sizable amount of time to clarifying one's Jewish identity, then life among the gentiles drags one down, leading one to a feeling that there is no need to preserve the Jewish People, especially not in a world that seems like a small "global village".

Precisely there, on alien soil, I felt more strongly than ever the need to preserve steadfastly the character of our unique people, both for our own sakes and for the sake of the entire world. Obviously, it is forbidden to despair. Chanuka teaches us that there always remains one small vessel of oil in every Jew, a small vessel capable of illuminating the lives of the individual and the nation.

On Shabbat, there were about thirty-five men and women at services, of whom about fifteen were converts, striving steadfastly to keep all the mitzvot. What leads non-Jews in Tucson to undergo a long, complex conversion process and to live as Jews? What brings them into the bosom of Judaism at a time when Jews are assimilating at such a high rate?

Gabriel converted with his wife and one of his sons. He told me that years ago he had lived in an area inhabited chiefly by Jews, Mexicans and people from India, so they had thought about the faiths of the nations, conducted clarifications and studied. They were exposed to Judaism and they underwent Reform conversion.

Yet they did not feel entirely comfortable with that conversion and they continued looking for the real thing, until they came upon a rabbi in Tucson and underwent conversion after two years of study. He and his wife and his son were united in their search and in their decision to convert. One of the daughters did not convert. "I think our miracle, that we converted together, I, my wife and my son, was greater than the miracle of your son," he said. It was hard for me to disagree with him.

My wife and I went to do some shopping for our grandchildren. A mother and father live through their children. Grandparents live through their grandchildren as well.

In the middle of shopping, my cell phone rang.

"Come quick. Aharon is having convulsions," said Tzvia, worried and alarmed. We left all our shopping in the middle of the store and raced to the apartment. It was an ominous feeling, and we were enormously worried.

We arrived at the apartment. Aharon was starting to come out of it. We ordered an American ambulance. About eight paramedics arrived and checked Aharon. The more time passed, the more Aharon recovered. He began joking at our expense and at the expense of the Red Cross team, who played along.

Thank G-d, we had been blessed with enormous miracles with Aharon, but not everything was yet perfect. We continued to pray to G-d, who had shown us many miracles until now, to continue bringing Aharon a complete recovery.

Thursday Night, the sixth night of Chanuka, we were invited to a Chanuka party of the Israeli community in Tucson. Every other year they hadn't been particular about having a kosher party, but this time they made the effort and made reservations at the kosher restaurant so we, too, would be able to eat. I did not know what to expect from that meeting, but we were told that such meetings give strength to the Israelis and connect them to our land and to our people.

We arrived at the party. Israelis, young and old, surrounded us. We saw their excitement and their interest and heard their offers of help. They didn't just offer help. They begged us to call them and ask for help. "Even something small for you would be something big for us."

Some of them had already been in Tucson for thirty years, and some, for two years. There were children amongst them who spoke Hebrew and others who spoke only English. It hurts to see that Jews do not feel that their place is in the Land of the Jews. On the one hand, the Israeli expatriates talk about their not having felt their Jewishness when they were in Eretz Yisrael, whereas in the Exile they feel more Jewish because they are connected to the Jewish community. On the other hand, this feeling is not enough to ward off their assimilation.

As I have already said, not everything we see and feel on the surface is what is really happening beneath the surface.

One couple there turned out to be distant relatives of Chaya, my wife. It's been said that when two Jews meet and don't find some family connection, it's a sign that they didn't talk long enough. The husband, Tidhar, a metal craftsman, explained to me excitedly that he had read all that had happened to Aharon and that a miracle was involved. "It could only be from Heaven." He told me that yesterday he had shown his son red blood cells through a special microscope. "Everything that happens to a single red blood cell is a great miracle. It has to be that this is not coincidental."

"Very interesting," I thought. "A secular Jew who lives in the United States, far from the Jewish community and from what is happening in Israel, does not believe that there could be a "bizarre coincidence", the term used by the newsman about the miracles of Cast Lead. For this Jew, it is obvious that a miracle is involved.

They invited us to go on a picnic with them on Sunday in a lovely park. They don't keep kosher, but they were careful to ask us what they could buy for us and where, so we would be able to eat as well. We toured the breathtaking scenery that characterizes Arizona in general and Tucson in particular. There was a gigantic desert there, containing flora and fauna unique to such a desert climate. The symbol of Arizona is the gigantic "savanna cactus". It has a tall trunk that can reach five or six meters or more, and a few branches coming out of the trunk. Its interior is almost entirely hollow. America.

Minor Celebrations

Just before the first operation came Aharon and Tzvia's first wedding anniversary. It had been a year of an unexpected and unconventional reality.

Everyone would ask us, "Where did you find your strength?" G-d only knows. It certainly wasn't easy, and it still isn't.

There in the distant exile we tried to improvise an evening party to mark their anniversary. We ordered special fish portions and a festive cake, and we decorated the apartment we were living in. I went to pick up the food from the only kosher butcher shop in Tucson. As I was getting ready to pay, a woman about thirty approached me and said in Hebrew, "You are the pride of us all." Who did she mean by "you"? Who did she mean by "us all". I had no way of clarifying who the woman was, and where she was from. She quickly disappeared.

My cell phone rang: "Hi Grandpa! Mazel tov! You've got another baby granddaughter." On the other end was our son Yair. We had hoped his wife would give birth while we were still in Israel. Yet Someone wanted differently, and the appropriate time turned out to be Tuesday, December 22.

It was a bizarre feeling. We were so far away from our children and from the new mother. It was something we were not used to. We were accustomed to being intimate participants in our children's lives, and certainly on special occasions. Such times are times of great joy, whether it involves bringing new life into the world, a new granddaughter, or restoring Aharon to renewed life. Thank G-d that we were privileged to be busy with the productive, constructive part of life.

The First Operation

Tuesday at 5:00 AM we were getting organized to head towards the hospital. The operation was supposed to start at 7:30 AM, and the physician estimated it would last about four or five hours. We looked at Aharon's "nose (not!)" and we knew this would be the last time we would see Aharon without it. Aharon, as a result of the injury, was left without a nose, and with three air passages. In this operation, they would take skin and tissue from his forehead, ear, ribs and foot, and they would begin to reconstruct his nose. The anesthesiologist, Dr. Adler, introduced himself. We understood that he was a Jew. Immediately after that a female physician who works in the hospital arrived and introduced herself to us as a former Israeli. She was prepared to accompany Aharon during the operation. We were starting to feel like we were in familiar surroundings.

At 7:30 the operation began. I felt as though the stranger the surroundings, the deeper and longer the prayers should be.

We were the only people in the waiting room who were praying. People were passing hours of waiting time, talking or in silence. There seemed to be no such thing as prayer in that hospital.

That's how it was with all the operations we experienced in the Tucson hospital. The non-Jews apparently pray only during their set prayer times. They watched us mumbling something to ourselves out of a small book. It was the verses of the psalms of David, King of Israel, which link up those who fervently recite them to spiritual powers and to energies that do not derive from the material world. "Though I walk through the valley of the shadow of death, I shall fear no evil, for You are with me" (Psalm 23:4). They watched us with wonderment. In an interview with the media about a month before the operation, Aharon had said that he felt like G-d was walking with him and with Tzvia everywhere, and he called that "a good, special feeling".

I recited King David's words, "L-rd, You brought me up from *She'ol*, preserved me from going down into the Pit" (Psalm 30:4). What a pit, what a *she'ol* Aharon had been in a year previous, and we with him! And what a fulfillment we had merited of the verse, that the Master-of-the-Universe had raised us up out of Sheol and restored Aharon's life. Our life!

After five hours we were expecting the doctor to come out to us. After five-and-a-half hours, they informed us that the doctor had conveyed that everything was fine, but that the operation would go on for about another hour. After seven hours the doctor emerged and informed us that the operation was over and that he was satisfied. He explained in detail the whole process, simultaneously so amazing and bizzarre. We had been expecting to see Aharon, but we would have to wait another hour-and-a-half. It was their practice not to allow people into the recovery room. While waiting, I received an email with pictures of the new granddaughter born just the day before. What a unique, amazing miracle! Just one day before, she had not been in our world, and here she was, an infant with hands, legs, a heart, kidneys and even a nose. At that very moment, Aharon was in an operation to reconstruct the nose that had disappeared as though it had never existed.

After nine hours, we saw Aharon. Aharon with a nose. That's right, it had two nostrils and a bridge. The nose was swollen, round, not yet fixed up. It looked as though it had been taken from anti-Semitic illustrations of the Jewish nose. In the operations to come, they would fix up the nose, albeit after almost a year in which we had gotten used to Aharon without it, and presumably we could get used to the strange nose as well. In his forehead a furrow had been dug out, from which the skin and tissue had been taken. The doctor said that slowly, the furrow would close up.

On Thursday we returned with Aharon from the hospital to the apartment, and we examined the physician's work of art. We were used to seeing numerous stitches in Aharon's head and in his other organs, Generally, the stitches were rough and protuberant. Here they were exceedingly delicate from the two sides of the nose, and from the nose in the direction of the forehead. The top part of the nose was still only lying on the outside, attached to the forehead. Gradually, Aharon was recuperating. Even the pain was starting to abate.

The physician wanted to examine Aharon again on the Sabbath. We explained that it would be hard for us to come for the examination on foot. "Is "Friday possible?" we asked. The doctor thought for a moment and nodded his head yes. We recalled the date, and asked him, "But what about Christmas?" The previous evening, in America, they would be celebrating Christmas, marking the birth of the man in whose name millions of Jews had been massacred. The doctor smiled and asked us to come at 10:00 AM. for the examination.

We received notice of a terror attack in the area of Shavei Shomron in Samaria. Following a relatively long cessation, a Jew had once more been killed in our ongoing war to return to our land and to live there. It is so hard to hear these tidings, especially when you are far from Israel and a bit cut off from it. The pace of our lives and of the lives of our people is astounding. Over and over, we move back and forth between joy and sadness, between successes and failures.

Someone was knocking at the door, which was quite out of the ordinary in the apartment we were staying in, especially since it was quite late, and on Friday Night at that. We had already finished our Friday Night meal, in which we had discussed the story of Joseph and his brothers. In that story, it turned out in the end that such a tragic story ultimately saved the lives of Jacob's family.

I peaked through the eyehole and saw a young man with a large earring in his ear. I tried to recall whether or not I knew him. I had a faint recollection of his being the fellow who had arrived on the spur of the moment to Friday Night services.

I opened the door. The young fellow explained that he had seen me in the synagogue, and only afterwards had recalled that I was the father of the wounded officer. He had looked for someone who could explain to him where we were living. He was excited, and he presented himself as Alon from Bat Yam, and he told us that he, too, had fought as a reservist in Cast Lead.

On Saturday Night he arrived again and he showed us pictures he had taken during the military operation. He was trying his luck financially in Tucson, like many other young people

"What are you missing in Israel?" I asked him. His answer was vague. As I have already said, some people leave the Land of Israel, and others enter it. I call America "the land of the show". On the surface, there are a lot of bells and whistles. Alon sells spices in one of the malls and is thinking of stopping and opening his own stall. "The work is very hard and the pay is low. Everyone dreams of opening their own stall," he said, and he too dreams of this.

That Saturday Night I took a look at the Internet and discovered that I.D.F. forces had killed the terrorists who had committed the terror attack two days before. Alon, the Israeli stall merchant in Tucson came to us again to offer help if we needed it.

This news item made a big impression on us. With all of Israel's problems, if anyone needed proof of how important a Jewish State is for us, both in security terms and in spiritual terms, here in the Exile I had learned about the spiritual tragedy of the Exile and about the tremendous security capability of the State of Israel.

Sunday was the public fast of the Tenth of Tevet, the Hebrew date on which Jerusalem's fall began during the First Temple Period. On the Ninth of Av, we mark Jerusalem's destruction, even though the seeds of that destruction had been planted beforehand. The Tenth of Tevet expresses the tragedy of the removal of G-d's regime and the attempt to say that that precisely man is exclusive master of reality. In our prayers we say, "Take pity on Your people and have mercy on Your inheritance."

"You know what?" asked Aharon, surprised and perplexed. "I touch my nose and I feel something on my forehead," and we rolled with laughter. Monday Morning we arrived at the doctor's office. He was very pleased with the results and with Aharon's condition. I said to him, "Aharon touches his nose and feels it . . ." and the doctor finishes my sentence with a smile, "on the forehead". He explained to us that until the last operation, the nose will be connected to the forehead, so the sensations of Aharon's nose would be in his forehead. What can you say? Such are the wonders of nature and of medicine. We set a date with the doctor for the next operation in another month and a week.

Tuesday Morning, we attended our last prayer service in the Tucson synagogue. When we came to the recitation of the "Shema", Aharon recited the first line out loud and then began to recite the rest in a loud whisper with the tune used in reading the Torah. I shed tears, hiding that from Aharon by covering my head with my prayer shawl. Before the injury, Aharon would recite the three paragraphs in a whisper and that same tune. Since the injury, he had not resumed that practice, or at least I hadn't heard it. Now I was privileged once more to hear it, and I was very excited. For me, this was one more sign that Aharon was getting back to his old self.

Things you see from there you don't see from here.

In Phoenix we boarded the plane for Israel, this time with a nose for Aharon. The nose was not particularly aesthetic, but it did have two nostrils. The airport security check was insane. Just the previous week a terrorist had been caught with an explosive belt on a plane in the United States. We were checked again and again. In one security check, a policewoman decided that Aharon was suspicious. They took him aside and began to examine him from head to toe. I, too, was privileged to undergo such a check the moment before boarding the plane. Not just in our country do we suffer from terrorists. Terrorists affect the whole world.

We had a stopover in New York. We had ten hours until the flight to Israel. A Jew who answers to the name of Ari came to take us for rest and a meal in his home, in the town of Lawrence. An acquaintance from our town, who had been wounded in the Yom Kippur War, made the connection. This was the first time I had ever met Ari. His hospitality was superb. His family had gone overboard to make our stay pleasant. Later on, an evening of appreciation of Aharon awaited us in the local synagogue. Dozens of people arrived to thank G-d for the miracle and to salute Aharon. Even in the United States, a year after the injury, people still got excited and set aside time to salute him.

We arrived back at the airport that night and stood in line once more to be checked. We could smell the Land of Israel. Once more people approached us, blessed us and saluted us. An older couple passed by and said, "We doff our hats to you." Another couple passed by and the husband asked-said, "I would like to hug you."

"Rabbi Zeev Karov! Hello!" said a Jew, dressed in Hareidi garb, with side-curls flowing down from his ears to his shoulders. I looked at him but I could not identify him. "I wouldn't be able to identify you either if I had not seen you in the media," he added.

"Well," I said, "Remind me, please."

"My name is Shmuel. We were in the same class in elementary school." Even though forty years had gone by, I remembered. He told me that he had been living in New York for twenty-five years, and that he belonged to a Hassidic court that was opposed to the Jewish State. We chatted a bit and then each of us turned back to making his own arrangements for the flight.

As we were in the business class lounge awaiting Aharon and Tzvia's flight, a man approached Aharon and said, "You're Aharon Karov, right?" Aharon answered in the affirmative." I own a cellular phone company and I will give you, free of charge, a cell phone for your trips abroad," declared the man, and he took Aharon's cell phone number.

The flight to Israel takes ten hours. An hour before landing, Shmuel approached my seat and asked to talk to me. He began by saying, "I ask that you not be humble here. If you merited such a big miracle, and you were privileged to sanctify G-d's name for the entire Jewish People, that's a sign that you've got heavenly merit." I still didn't understand what he wanted from me. "I want you to bless me. I've got a sick daughter and several other problems. Don't refuse. You've got merit."

I had already learned a lesson: There are times and situations in which all the outer shells of the Jewish People are nullified. Who would have believed that a Hareidi Jew who rejects the State of Israel would view Aharon's story, which is totally Zionistic and military, as something positive, and not only that, but that he would ask a blessing of Aharon's Zionist father?

"Is there a chance to mend the rift in our nation?" the headlines of our nation's newspapers frequently cry out, whenever something happens which attests to divisiveness. "Is there something that fuses together all parts of the nation?" Panels and meetings of party representatives deliberate on this issue. And here, in a night flight from New York to our little country, a Hareidi, a secular Jew and a fellow with a knitted yarmulke joined together to express their excitement and to salute an army officer wounded in a war defending our country.

We were flying at an altitude of ten thousand meters above the earth. What you see from above, you don't see from below. We were above the clouds, which looked like silent mountains of snow. When the plane was flying over the Atlantic, it looked as though the clouds and the sea were kissing each other.

I said to myself, "Everything depends on your perspective. From whence does each person gaze at his own life and at the reality?

A friend of mine, an army officer, sent me an article published in an I.D.F. officers' journal, "*Ma'arachot*". The article dealt with soldiers' motivation to fight in Operation Cast Lead. "Read this and send them a response," he vociferously instructed me. I read it and was filled with sorrow. In the article, titled "Research Study", three researchers asked hundreds of soldiers what made them fight and endanger their lives in the war. The soldiers could choose one of seven possibilities. Not one nationalist or values-related choice was offered amongst the answers. What answers did appear? Hatred of the enemy, lack of a choice, friends, and several other similar responses. The possibilities did not include "defending the residents of the South" or "defending the homeland". The article was an insult to the intelligence, and, obviously, misleading as well, and sure enough, I wrote an article in response.

I mentioned that Aharon, his own soldiers and many other soldiers spoke about the lights of Sderot and the residents of the South as what motivated them to fight. I mentioned things said by parents of wounded soldiers about the necessity of restoring the country's honor, and the need to stop the humiliation of the Jewish People, who had been bombarded from Gaza for seven years. I also wrote that it is important to understand that not everything you see and hear superficially is what is really happening beneath the surface. People can cite reasons that motivate them to do this or that action, but they lack the ability to express the real reason, or, the real reason lies in their subconscious. Any fledgling psychologist will tell you that a small child who makes trouble is really looking for love.

How important it is the way we look at reality and the way we analyze what we see and what we hear.

Our First Banquet of Thanksgiving

The one-year Hebrew anniversary of the injury arrived, 17 Tevet (the English anniversary, January 13, was still ten days off). Every time we had thought about holding a banquet in thanks to G-d for the miracles He had performed for Aharon and for us, something came up to delay it, unexpected surgery or something else. Now a whole year had gone by, and besides our daily thanks, we felt the need to do something more official. It was therefore decided that we would hold a large banquet with many invitees at the end of the series of operations.

As noted, the first Hebrew anniversary of the injury was 17 Tevet, which fell out on a Sunday. We decided that one day before, we would hold a banquet of thanksgiving for the immediate family, i.e., Aharon's siblings, Tzvia's siblings, the parents and the two grandmothers. The total number of participants would be forty. On Thursday we arrived home from the first operation in Arizona, and the meal was set for Saturday Night, just two days later. Obviously, the program and food were therefore organized by the siblings, who called us in Tucson when they needed advice.

The Shabbat before the meal one of my sons asked me, "Why not wait with the meal until Aharon finishes all the operations?" For me it was very important to thank G-d before the operations were completed. Since Aharon's injury we had constantly tried to see the good, even if it was only partial. I felt that giving thanks after everything was completed was no great feat. Rather, it was important to give thanks for the miracles G-d had already performed, precisely at a time when we were still struggling with problems and difficulties.

Yet why precisely on the day of Aharon's injury did we celebrate the miracles he had experienced in his return to life? Would it not have been more appropriate to hold such a banquet on the anniversary of the day he began to walk or to talk once more? Yet we believe that on the day of Aharon's injury, the seeds of his salvation were already sown. We still had to pray and the physicians still had to perform their work steadfastly. Yet the potential for success was already sown on the day of the injury. As our sages said, "On the day of the Temple's destruction, the Messiah was born." The Creator of the Universe plants the possibility of salvation deep within the trouble itself.

8:00 PM Saturday Night the family was slowly assembling. Every one of those present took turns expressing the overwhelming feeling that we had experienced a great miracle. It was not within the human ability to produce such life forces and such powers of perseverance. "It was the L-rd's doing" (Psalm 118:23). Yes, both the suffering and the deliverance, both the injury and the unique recovery we had experienced and to which we still bore witness.

Aharon pointed out that he was experiencing daily. It wasn't just the fact that he was alive. The improvements in his sight, in his right hand, in his speech; his new-old nose, and, obviously, his anticipation of a new birth – all this and more was happening every moment.

Aharon, Tzvia and my wife Chaya took turns reciting the blessing of "*HaGomel*", recited when one survives a dangerous experience, and praising G-d for "bestowing favors on the undeserving". Their blessings included thanks for their safely weathering transcontinental flights, as well as for Aharon's successful operation. Immediately afterwards, Ruthy, wife of my son Ya'ir, likewise recited it for the childbirth experience she had just undergone safely, a birth that had produced our new granddaughter, Tal. Thank G-d, one joyous occasion touches on the next, and one life is followed by another.

Each person reciting the blessing was stating that we are not perfect. We know we are undeserving. We are indebted to the world. Yet despite that G-d did us a good turn.

Each time someone recited the blessing, those assembled responded in turn, "May He who has shown you every kindness ever deal kindly with you."

Aharon spoke as well. He thanked the Master-of-the-Universe for the life-forces that had been uncovered in him. He thanked the parents and the entire family.

Since his birth, Aharon had never been a man of words, and since the injury he had obviously spoken little, also because speaking was difficult. This time, Aharon spoke for about twenty-five minutes.

"Since your birth, I cannot recall hearing you speak at such length," I told Aharon. One of the rabbis who was asked to speak about Aharon's restored speech faculties said that it had been obvious to him that Aharon would start speaking again. "Why?" he was asked.

"Because the verse testifies: 'Aharon shall surely speak'" (Exodus 4:14), he answered. "This verse relates to Aharon, the High Priest, who was lover of peace and who pursued peace. Aharon the High Priest's most important characteristic involved his speech. First and foremost, he made use of his speech faculty to make peace between people and to bring them together. He would approach someone in a dispute and say to him, 'You know how much your friend wants to make up with you, but he is too embarrassed,' and he would say the same to the other person, and thanks to him, they would make up."

Monday Evening I received a call from Aharon and Tzvia. They sounded distraught. "Aharon was showering and the whole scab from his forehead fell off." We asked them to photograph it and to send us the picture by email. The wonders of technological development. We looked at it and to laymen like us it looked all right. Yet we decided to send the pictures to the doctor in Tucson. An hour later the answer arrived from Tucson. "Everything seems to be all right. This is part of the recovery process."

Interim Report

January 13, 2010 the secular anniversary arrived. My mother called and informed me, "Channel 10 is broadcasting a program about the rehabilitation of Ben Schpitzer. Go see it."

Ben was very severely wounded and he, too, had hovered between life and death. For about half a year Aharon and Ben had shared a room in Beilinson Hospital and in Tel HaShomer Hospital. Ben's rehabilitation was difficult and complicated, and Ben and his parents had a hard time dealing with it. Their style is rough and unpolished, but they are full of Israeli resilience and faith. I knew them already, but I was still surprised by the power of Ben's responses. Ben said:

"Before entering Gaza they asked if anybody wants to leave and not go in. I know that even had I been certain I would be wounded and they had shown me how I would look now, I wouldn't have left. I would have gone in and fought,"

The interviewer asked "Why?" and Ben's simple answer was, "Because they needed me."

Later in the interview Ben was asked about his future plans: "What are you thinking about doing with the rest of your life?" Ben answered without hesitation: "If they let me, I'll go back to the army to lecture to young soldiers. That would make me very happy. If not, I'll go study psychology."

"Psychology?" asked the interviewer. "That's what you want?"

"Yes," answered Ben. "To help others."

I heard this and I started to cry. "True cast lead!" I thought to myself. Under the rough veneer lies a gentle soul who wants to contribute and to give to others. No one can tell me that the power of goodness and unity in my people, the power I was exposed to wherever I went during the past year, does not exist. What sort of person can tell me that there is no truth to the saying that deep down, we are all the children of Abraham, that bastion of kindness, and that we all wish not to be egotistical? Ben Schpitzer seemingly had all the reasons in the world to say, "Everyone can go to the devil. I'm only going to worry about myself." Yet instead he said, "Even had I known I would be wounded, I would have gone into Gaza, because I am helping my people."

I recalled that when I was praying in Tucson out of a prayer book with an English translation and commentary, I saw a marvelous explanation. There it stated that the essence of our prayers is the Shemoneh Esreh, the Eighteen benedictions, recited silently. The first blessing is called "*Avot*"-The Patriarchs. That blessing ends with the words, "Shield of Abraham". That English commentary explained that G-d shields Abraham's character trait of kindness so that it remains rooted in each and every one of us.

Once more a faint, hidden voice within me asked, "And why is that trait only rarely revealed?" Only G-d knows. Yet, continuing my inner dialogue I asked myself: "Would you want to live in a perfect world in which man has nothing to do, a world in which man has no problems to cope with?"

Again and again, I found myself encountering the hard side of life. I consoled mourners, a family whose twenty-year-old son was killed. Every parent feels deep within that his children are his life's essence. To lose a child is the hardest experience one can cope with in life.

I sat myself down by the father and was silent. What can I say to a father who buried his son yesterday? The father initiated our conversation: "We learned from you how one deals with great difficulties," the father said in tears. Once more I was having trouble absorbing what had been said. How could he possibly compare the hardships? What had he learned from us about his situation?

Some defined our method of coping as naïve, as repressing the reality. Was this father, as well, naïve? Was he, too, trying to repress reality?

I read an interview with the brothers of Gavriel Hoter, murdered in the Otniel Yeshiva together with three more of his friends. They put out a song disc in memory of their brother. They were asked, "The Musical Group "Friends of Natashe" sings, 'I don't dance when I'm sad.' Don't you feel that you've got to stop singing due to the sadness and pain over your brother's death?" They answered, "There are moments that are not easy. Yet Rabbi Shlomo Carlebach showed us that it is possible and necessary to sing in every situation."

Really? Is that, as well, not a case of repression and naivety?

Veteran Israel actor Yosef Graber was interviewed on the radio. During my childhood, Graber lived on Ben Yehuda Street in Tel Aviv, and our balconies faced each other. The Cameri Theater was putting on a new show – "Tuesdays with Morrie". He explained his role as Morrie, as well as that of the boy Yiftach, whom he was trying to educate, and he said, "I think the problem Yiftach is dealing with is the problem of today's youth. The race to earn a living and to gain advancement at work, as well as the constant need to meet contemporary cultural expectations, leave one with no time to reflect, to think, to encounter his own soul."

Obviously, this is not a problem of youth, but a problem of society at large. I recall what Azriel Carelebach wrote in his book *India*. He joined up with an American delegation going to India. Inter alia, they showed Indian ministers a film about life in the U.S. The film showed a man who was just starting out, with a meager salary, and living in a very small apartment. After some time, he was earning more and could allow himself to move to a more spacious apartment. Still later he has already purchased a car, and he then bought a summer home, and so on and so forth.

Carlebach related that at the end of the film one of the Indian ministers approached him and asked, "Tell me, is that really how things are? They're never satisfied? When do they have time to be happy and to rest?"

Unfortunately, that's how life is in western culture. It is a culture that has not passed over our little land. Obviously this culture has positive things about it, as well, but we've gone too far. I, too, have sensed this during the last year in the race towards Aharon's recovery. Occasionally I had to stop to think deeply and to take it all in, and to let things just pass me by.

"Dad," said Aharon, "I'm being pressured to talk about the injury and to offer encouragement to boys before their army induction. I think the time has come for me to talk."

Since the reports from two months previous in the *Yediot Aharonot* Newspaper and on Channel 2, there had been non-stop requests for Aharon to give talks: in yeshiva high schools; regular high schools; to Bnei Akiva youth groups; in the army; and at all sorts of conventions. More and more they were turning to him and to me with requests for talks. Aharon could not say yes. First of all, he still had trouble speaking. True, his speech was constantly improving, yet the words still did not come out every time he needed them. Second of all, as opposed to Aharon the High Priest, whose "profession" was speech, our Aharon was a man of deeds and not a man of words, at least until now.

Aharon's present readiness to speak represented another step in his return to full health. Still another revival of the dead.

The next morning I received a call from the head of the *Ma'ag-alim* organization, which provides workshops on identity and motivation in high schools. "I would like to ask if I might invite Aharon to give a talk to our counselors. He can give them a lot of strength." I explained that there was a chance that it would work out. "Call at the start of next week," I said. He immediately went on decisively, "We are willing to provide Aharon with office services that might help him to organize his talks and facilitate his arrival at them." Without missing a beat I stopped the flow of his words: "Take it slow! Aharon is not turning his talks into a profession nor even to an avocation that will take up many hours. At least not in the near future." I ended the conversation and felt contentment. How good it felt to know that we had reached the point of having such conversations about Aharon.

My cell phone rang and the number on the screen indicated a call from the United States. "This is Bat Sheva. Representatives of the Israeli consulate at Tucson contacted me and they want to interview you for the Jewish newspaper. Can we set a date?" she asked, almost decreeing. "I'll talk with Aharon and Tzvia and get back to you," I said.

Everyone who talks to us about this thinks that these interviews are important and provide strength to their readers. Is it really so? In any event, for us it isn't a simple matter to respond to every such request, and it is certainly many times as hard for Tzvia and Aharon.

Tu Bishvat, the holiday of trees, arrived. That day marks our faith in flowering and rebirth. When one plants a seed in the earth, it rots and gradually disappears. Yet that is just what one sees on the surface, or via a microscope. Precisely through the process of the seed's "demise" new life is born. The stalk will ultimately surface and flower there in the soil.

The Second Operation

On a Saturday Night in early February, thirteen months after the injury, Aharon and Tzvia flew to New York before continuing on to Tucson for the second operation. Both we and they had received numerous offers of lodgings and hospitality. Jews from Israel and from abroad were interested in helping them in their stay. Jews take responsibility for one another. A week later, my wife Chaya joined them, flying to Tucson.

The morning of the operation, the physician explained that for two hours he would continue fixing up the nose and then for two hours he would work on the lips. He would take from the lower lip to use in the upper lip, and in the end the lips would be perfect. Just as he had said that the forehead would fix itself, so did he say about what was missing from the lip. And sure enough, the forehead had become perfect, the cleft disappearing. Tissue was reformed and only the skin needed more time to conceal the wound. Presently, the forehead wound looked like that of a child who fell while playing basketball and scraped his forehead.

I remained in Israel, receiving constant phone updates. That was very hard. This was the first time since the injury that I was not by Aharon during an operation. Several minutes before the operation I spoke to Aharon. We offered each other encouragement. The operation began at 7:30 AM, Tucson time. Here in Israel it was nine hours later – 4:30 PM.

This time we thought the operation would be short, but experience is the best teacher, and we were prepared for a long operation as well. This was a painstaking operation requiring caution, precision and patience. It involved taking small pieces from all sorts of places in the body and rebuilding the nose and lips anew.

The operation took over six hours. At 2:00 PM, Tucson time, the operation was over. Two hours later I called my wife to receive a situation report. She was with Aharon in the recovery room. In a whisper she reported that, thank G-d, the doctor was satisfied, and that Aharon was starting to wake up. Suddenly I heard Aharon say, "Mom, I'll talk to Dad." I was surprised. In the previous operation, it had taken Aharon a long time to wake up. What is more, this time, the doctors had operated on his lips, as well. In the days to come, he could expect to have a hard time opening his mouth.

"Dad, don't worry, everything is excellent," I heard Aharon's voice, loud and determined. With Aharon, "Everything is excellent" means that he is suffering pain, but it isn't bothering him too much. Every individual should accustom himself to seeing beneath the surface and to hearing what stands behind the words that are uttered on the surface.

Once more, I was shocked by Aharon's strengths, by his fierce desire to calm us. How fortunate we were!

True Strength

Aharon shared a dilemma with us: Should he address battle shock victims and wounded whose recovery is slow and difficult? Obviously, I recommended that he do it. I had already learned that lessons are not learned conventionally through the brain. People become stronger through those who have demonstrated true strength.

I discovered that numerous educational institutions were

showing Aharon's Channel 2 interview. A year and two months after the injury, numerous, varied requests were still being made to us. For example, the Eilat municipality asked Aharon to address local high school students. Moreover, one of the people in charge of the International Bible Contest on Israel Independence Day asked that Aharon's story be broadcast during the contest, and that Aharon ask one of the questions there.

Right after Purim, I flew to Poland with a delegation of students from the yeshiva. On the plane I asked myself: This time around, will the visit be different for me?

There's something new with every delegation. In Birkenau, we stood on the famous ramp where Mengele and the officers made their selection – who for life and who for death. Every time I had been there before, I felt as though it were cursed and terrible. We stood in a circle around the guide who was explaining what happened in those dark days. I took several steps away from the group to think. Suddenly, I heard the group calling for quiet: "Shhhh . . .". I approached and I heard Tzvi Florental, father of one of the students, reciting a blessing: "Blessed are You, O G-d . . . who performed a miracle for my fathers in this place."

I shook my head in disbelief, wondering how someone could recite a blessing in such a terrible place as this, and such an optimistic blessing, so steeped in faith, as that one. Sure enough, Tzvi's mother had been saved by her own resourcefulness. She was spared in the selection and afterwards as well in the disrobing room before the gas chamber, because both times they suddenly were ordered to leave.

"The world is very complex," I said to myself. "In such a dark place, there were also points of light." We continued walking. As we stood above the ruins of the crematorium we spoke by telephone with Tzvi's mother. "My revenge is that you are standing there with the flag of Israel," she concluded, after telling us her story from those dark days.

Wednesday we were in the Children's Forest, where an estimated 800 children, cruelly murdered in the town of Tarnov, are buried in a mass grave. That's right! My feelings run deep here. They are different. When your son is fighting for his life, the feeling is very harsh and profound. Now here I was, standing by the grave of children who did not survive. The feeling, so natural, that our children are our whole life, did not help these children when exposed to the darkest side of man.

I tears, I told the students: "Don't be confused by this terrible wickedness. The world has a lot of good, even if there is not a little wickedness as well. G-d gave man free will to decide whither he takes the enormous resources given to him."

In the Auschwitz gas chamber one of the students sobbed and asked/shouted: "Shall I take pictures and show my grandmother where her entire family was murdered?" I hugged him and said, "Yes! Show your grandmother where her family was murdered. Show her, as well, your picture with the flag of Israel in this gas chamber."

For our sakes, they turned off the lights in the gas chamber. We closed our eyes and tried to imagine what those Jews who died there had experienced during those cursed moments. Together we recited, "Hear O Israel! Hashem is our G-d! Hashem is one!" A shudder pervaded my whole body. The contrast between then and now, between good and evil, between those who were privileged to carry on and those who were not, shook me to the core. I recalled reciting the "Shema" several minutes before receiving the news about Aharon's injury.

The night before our return to Israel, one of the students said, "I have never recited Hallel on Israel Independence Day. This year, I will recite it and even shout the blessing."

Two weeks before Pesach, Hamas launched Kasam Missiles from Gaza. One of them killed a Thai worker. "Don't you think Operation Defensive Shield was senseless?" I was asked. Sometimes I think the expression "senseless" is a favorite of quite a few people in our country. Senseless wars. Senseless car accidents, etc., etc. True, I had thought Cast Lead should be continued and the heads of Hamas in Gaza should be liquidated, but I do not think and did not think it would end the cycle of violence or nullify the fact that "in every generation they rise up against us to destroy us." We have been fighting for our country since its inception, and in the Exile we ceaselessly fought for our survival. Defending the residents of the South constituted a national imperative, and smiting the evildoers constituted a moral imperative. Operation Defensive Shield performed both, albeit imperfectly. I am not aware of one war that Israel executed to perfection. We were always forced to keep on fighting afterwards, to keep on defending our lives. Even after the Egyptian exodus we were sometimes subject to others, and even after the War of Independence and the Six Day War we were forced to fight every several years.

Saturday Night, the first night of Pesach, we heard about two soldiers killed in Gaza. Yes, the war was going on. A regiment deputy commander of the Golani Infantry Brigade had been killed. The horrifying news item announced that his brother had been killed twelve years previous in Lebanon. How does a mother cope with bereavement over her two sons? It is unfathomable. I read what the mother said after her initial cries of despair over the awful news:

"Peretz recounted that her four sons had served in a crack unit of the Golani Brigade, "*Sayeret Golani*": 'I don't know what *Sayeret Golani* is, but I know that G-d loves the *Sayeret Golani* of the Peretz family. He loves those fighters. He loves my Eliraz – a true war hero, a boy who longed for a meaningful life. He didn't have a single meaningless moment in his whole life. Every moment of his life was aimed at service on behalf of the Jewish People,' said Peretz. She added that no mother, not on the Israeli side and not on the Palestinian side, wants her children to die. Even so, she taught her children to live proudly in Eretz Yisrael. 'Life in this land is acquired through pain. Eliraz did not set out to die, but to ensure that you and I can live here. He was killed for the sake of us all, so that we could walk in pride,' said the mother."

A mother forged of cast lead. Yes, there are still other upright, idealistic people who are not confounded even by the worst news. Without a doubt, the pain of a mother who has lost her son is unbearable. It's obvious that a father who sees his son suffer greatly suffers as well. Yet there is no contradiction between that pain and suffering, on the one hand, and between having faith and viewing reality positively on the other. I salute such a mother with all my heart and soul. Apparently, there are many like her, more than we tend to believe.

The next day, the media broadcast the mother's words from the funeral. As her son's body was being covered with dirt, she continued to be herself. Like two people in one, you could hear in her voice the profound, unfathomable pain and you could hear in her voice the fortitude and faith.

Once more the media was asking where this faith came from. Once more they were trying to attribute that cast-lead strength to individuals. I think I have learned, however. This strength belongs to the entire nation. Amongst a few it is expressed mightily. Amongst others it is not revealed at all. There are times when it bursts forth and appears without warning and there are times when it remains hidden, yet it always exists deep within us.

In times such as these in which some people are panicking over the pressure from the United States as far as building in Jerusalem, there are those who know how to stand erect and to reveal fortitude even when their sons are killed.

An Unconventional Flight

Following deliberation it was decided to push off the third operation until a week after Pesach. The operation was set for April 13, precisely a year and three months after the injury. This meant we wouldn't be in Israel for Israel Independence Day and would be forced to celebrate it in the exile. This time we'd be flying without Tzvia. She was already in advanced pregnancy, and flying then is not recommended.

By now we were getting accustomed to the new routine in our lives. True, we had resumed normal life: work, family, society and the State of Israel. At the same time, within that one routine was embedded yet another: medical appointments and consultations with doctors; surgical operations in Israel and abroad. Without noticing it, this new regimen had already been in place for a year and two months.

Routine was both a friend and an enemy. It afforded our lives security – I knew what was happening and where my life was headed. Routine made us professionals in all our pursuits.

Yet that routine also put a damper on our quality of life, robbing life of its meaning. To think outside the box, to be renewed, to learn lessons, to ponder life deeply – all those things require an exit from routine. I felt that escaping the routine forced on us helped us to ponder our lives more fully, and allowed us to be refreshed.

Israel celebrated its sixty-second Independence Day. From the perspective of nations, Israel was very young. Yet in reality, our country has been through a great deal. Once more there were calls from the media. They wanted to film and interview us on Independence Day. We explained to everyone that unfortunately this year we would be forced to celebrate Independence Day in the exile.

We flew. We parted from Tzvia, who, as noted, was remaining in Israel this tiime. She was in the eighth month of her pregnancy. There was new life in her womb.

Once more we were flying. It is a long flight, a night flight lasting over fifteen hours. At the start of the night we flew over the skies of Israel and Europe, and we continued during the night hours to America.

Most of the travelers slept or tried to sleep. Yet such a quantity of hours allows for numerous interesting conversations with all sorts of people. On one of those occasions, when I got up from my seat to get a drink, one of stewards began a conversation with me.

"How is your son doing?" he asked. The steward was a young fellow with an earring in his ear and his entire head smoothly shaven. Had I been asked what I thought of him, his life and his values system, based on his outer appearance I probably would have given a certain type of answer. He felt a need to tell me about his life. "My father was a fighter pilot in the Air Force. In 1992 he was riding his motorcyle and a car hit him. He was thrown forcefully against an electric pole and mortally wounded. He lay for a long time in a coma, all his bones broken. My mother was pregnant. One day, while sitting by his bedside, I got a call announcing the birth of my brother. A number of hours later my father woke up. My parents called my newborn brother 'Chaim' [life].''

Obviously I am shortening the story, dear reader. Yet the key phrases I had heard so many times during the last year from all sorts of directions were uttered here as well: "I believe everything is from heaven. This story taught us to look at life differently. It's no coincidence that my father woke up right after my brother was born." This, and so many other such sentences point to something very profound taking place deep inside us.

Here, ten thousand meters above the earth, I was once more hearing, from someone ostensibly far removed from me in his worldview, that everything is from heaven. As I have already said, not everything visible on the surface is what is really happening beneath the surface.

I returned to my seat on the plane. Yet I couldn't sit down. My spot had been taken by a senior steward who was having a conversation with Aharon. "I wanted to talk with the 'celeb' and to hear about his situation and about what he'd been through," he explained to me, saying he was from Kibbutz Givat Chaim. "Undergoing what you have helps one to take life in perspective," he half asked, half said. And all this minutes after my hearing about Chaim, brother of the other steward.

I "patrolled" the plane with Aharon, and a yarmulke-clad man with a thick American accent asked Aharon, "You're the hero, right?" answering his own question. I chatted with him. I discovered that his story was that of much of the Jewish People. He had grown up in an assimilated family in Detroit. About eight years ago he had decided to move to Israel, and slowly he began becoming religious. He had to go abroad very often because he was fundraising for the important and gargantuan project of *Ir David*, the City of David. "Today," he said, "this is the third most popular tourist site after the Kotel and Masada." David, King of Israel, symbolized our people's past alongside our unending yearnings for a more perfect future. "David, King of Israel, lives and endures."

The project of bringing to rebirth the City of David was begun by a "nut" likewise named David, or "Dovidel" as he is called. Might this be a mere coincidence? To this very day, Dovidel continues developing the City of David. One nut has succeeded in changing the outlook of Israeli governments to the City of David, in Judaizing the site and in opening up for hundreds of thousands each year a portal on the Kingdom of Israel from ancient times.

Aharon succeeded in falling asleep for quite a while on the flight. I, by contrast, had a hard time doing the same. For a long time, I watched him sleeping. The sight excited me greatly. He was alive and breathing well, and was managing to sleep. Once in several long minutes he would shift himself to change his position. I never thought I would ever get excited over the sight of a twenty-four-year-old sleeping.

The next night, in the Tucson apartment, we tried to imagine and to guess how Aharon would look after the operation. Would his nose look exactly like a regular nose?

The Third Operation

Tuesday, a year and three months after the injury, we got up at five thirty AM, recited morning prayers like every other day, but to those prayers was obviously added a special prayer for the success of the operation that would begin two hours later. Every operation is accompanied by fears. Prolonged sedation is not recommended for a normal person, let alone for Aharon with the shrapnel in his brain. Moreover, operations always involve risks. Hence our prayer – that the operation should succeed and to bring us to our desired destination.

We arrived at the hospital at 6:15 AM. We already knew the hospital from the previous operations, but it still felt very alien to us. This was not our country and these were not our people.

Preparations were made for the operation. Dr. Menick arrived and we asked him, in the Israeli manner, to take the opportunity to carry out another wee little operation and to remove from Aharon's foot a piece of shrapnel that had been bothering him recently. As you may recall, Aharon's body was covered with hundreds of schrapnel pieces. Some of them were coming out over time, some would remain forever and some would torment him, and there would be a need for medical intervention to remove them.

To our great surprise, the doctor agreed. He took Aharon's signature on the removal of the schrapnel piece. Thank G-d, we succeeded in sparing Aharon one operation and a local anesthetic.

At 1:00 PM the physician emerged and said that he had completed the operation and was very pleased. It was a short operation compared to what we were used to, just three hours.

We joined Aharon in Recovery. He was groggy and was slowly reawakening. He had a nose like anybody else. True, it was a bit swollen, but it stood there on its own, was not connected to the forehead and was not strange.

"Aharon, touch your nose," I said to him. "What do you want me to do?" he asked, as though he could not understand. "Will you feel the touch on your nose or your forehead?" As noted, since the first nose operation, Aharon had been touching his nose but feeling it on his forehead. "I don't feel it on my forehead but on my nose," answered Aharon, happy and surprised.

We didn't jump for joy, but I sense that that was only due to the lengthy process involved in reconstructing the nose. We had already seen the nose's structure and gotten used to it gradually. Yet if you recall that previously he did not have any nose, and now he had a regular nose, you can understand what a great miracle was involved.

In the coming days, we would often see people's excitement over Aharon's nose and over the fact that when Aharon touched it, he felt his nose and not his forehead.

We used the wonders of technology to bring Tzvia, as well, closer to Aharon's new look. We called with Skype so Tzvia would see it. The wonders of technological development can contribute greatly to life, although, unfortunately, they can also corrupt and destroy.

Independence Day Abroad

Since Aharon felt well, we decided to fly to Los Angeles on Israel Independence Day. That city has a large community that celebrates the holiday. While Tucson has thirty thousand Jews, almost no one celebrates religious Jewish holidays, let alone national days like Israel Independence Day. I made contact the Israeli emissary of the Bnei Akiva Religious Zionist Movement in Los Angeles, and he immediately responded happily. They would come to the airport, pick us up and host us for as long as we wanted. Obviously, they immediately asked us to address the ceremony. "I'm used to making speeches," I told Shlomo, the Bnei Akiva emissary. "As for Aharon, we'll ask him the day before the ceremony and see how he feels."

The desire to talk, on the one hand, and the difficulty in speaking and in standing before an audience, on the other hand, had been troubling Aharon for some time. Now, as well, Aharon would grapple with the two sides and decide whatever he would decide. You needed a lot of strength to survive what Aharon had been through and was still going through, and he would know how to deal with these dilemmas as well.

Before flying to Los Angeles, we discovered that Tucson held a yearly Memorial Day ceremony, on the day before Independence Day. Those in the know described the yearly ceremony as a modest one. This year, however, our visit to the city had aroused an attempt to unite all the Jewish bodies for the ceremony. The head of the Tucson Israel Center invited us to participate in the ceremony and asked that Aharon light a torch in memory of the fallen.

We found about two hundred people at the ceremony. Most were recent or not-so-recent arrivals from Israel, emissaries of their Israeli work place or emissaries of themselves. The ceremony was, indeed, respectable and moving. Aharon dedicated his torch lighting to those individuals who had focused their lives on the Jewish People and their country, and not on themselves.

At the start of the ceremony, it was made clear to me in no uncertain terms that although we were in a Jewish compound at a Jewish-Israeli ceremony, we were still in the exile, subject to another regime. The ceremony began with a group of boys ascending the stage, placing their hands on their hearts and singing the American National anthem. That's right, even on Israeli Memorial Day, at a ceremony mourning our fallen, they were required in the Land of Democracy to sing the American anthem and to place their hands on their hearts. Is that or is that not the exile?

At the ceremony a film clip was shown about Michael Levin, who was killed in the Second Lebanon War. Michael moved to Israel by himself from Arizona, and was happy with that deed until the day he died. Obviously, the local Jewish paper also asked Aharon for an interview.

At the end of the ceremony, we went to a mall to look for a large hat for Aharon. Exposure to the sun after the operation was not good for his nose or forehead. We walked several meters and suddenly a young spice merchant approached us, asking, "Hebrew? Do you speak Hebrew?" We spoke a bit and continued on our way. A young woman who sold purses stopped us. "I know you," she said, struggling to recall. "Um, you're that fellow who was wounded in the war, right?" She did not wait for an answer. "Thank you very much! The best of health!"

Still another expression of thanks.

We moved on, trying to concentrate on the task at hand.

The next morning, we were at the doctor's for a follow-up exam. He removed stitches from Aharon's head and was happy with the appearance of his nose. We were happy that he was happy, and we raced to the apartment to pack up and to leave for Los Angeles. At the airport, a couple was waiting for us, and they took us to the apartment of a family that wholeheartedly went out of their way to spoil us. Several families shared in hosting us during those two days, and each did all they could to ensure that our stay would be pleasant.

Independence Day Eve we arrived at the largest synagogue in Los Angeles. About a thousand men, women and children had arrived to mark Memorial Day and Independence Day. A thousand people is very many, but I thought about the 120,000 Jews of Los Angeles and the 300,000 Israelis living in the area, and I wondered, "Where are they celebrating, if at all?"

We were invited up on stage to speak. The audience rose and clapped their hands for several minutes. Since Memorial Day the previous year, when we had participated in the Jerusalem International Convention Center ceremony, I cannot recall such a reception.

Aharon spoke of the need of each individual to make a contribution to the State of Israel, like the fallen who had placed the good of the Jewish People and State before their own personal lives. After the ceremony and the festive evening prayer, we remained there for a long time, shaking hands and hearing, over and over, "Thank you very much for agreeing to come to us," and, "Thank you very much, Aharon, for what you did." A year and three months had gone by, and people still grew excited on seeing Aharon and hearing his story.

Many people asked that the next time we came to Los Angeles we should be their guests. "We've got a lot of room in our home and we will take you to beautiful sites." I asked myself, "They're good Jews, and good Zionists, but why don't they move to the country of the Jews?" Not that it's such a simple matter, but still . . .

The next day we fulfilled the "mitzvah" of Israel Independence Day – holding a barbeque – at the home of Shlomo, the local Bnei Akiva emissary. He told us that an irreligious Jew (I don't like distinguishing between religious and irreligious Jews) wanted to invite us that evening to a restaurant to meet us.

"We're talking about a very special, interesting Jew," said Shlomo. That evening we arrived at a dairy restaurant, obviously with the strictest kashrut standards. The Jew, named Ari (interesting, the same name as the person who hosted us in New York on our first trip abroad), arrived with several other Jews thirsty for the State of Israel and desirous of a connection with Israelis. We had a long, interesting talk about the State of Israel, its virtues and shortcomings. Ari described the struggle he was trying to wage in the universities, which are awash with anti-Semitism and with poisonous propaganda against the State of Israel. "In the talk given by Colonel Bentzy Gruber last week, Muslims got up and started yelling. Only one person answered them. At the end of the lecture, we approached that person and it turned out to be a non-Jew, a Christian. The Jews here are afraid to answer them and confront them," he said. Bentzy Gruber is "five-star" reservist in Israel, contributing about half of each year to the army. We grew up together in the Tel Aviv of long ago. It's a small world, as I've already said.

Near the end of the meal, Ari's brother arrived. He was dressed in contemporary garb, with bracelets on his hands and a shaven head. "Get yourself a piece of cake," I said to him. "I ate meat so I can't eat dairy now," he answered. And I, like someone who does not learn from experience, was surprised. I forgot for a moment that not everything visible from the outside is really what can be found, living and breathing, beneath the surface.

Finally, we returned to Eretz Yisrael. On this flight, as on every other, Aharon received special treatment. One of the stewardesses related that from the moment of Aharon's injury until then, she had been praying every day for his recovery. Obviously, she was very excited to see him. The tumult surrounding Aharon led one of the passengers to approach me. He asked who we were, where we were from and what the tumult was about. "And where are you from?" I asked. "From Tucson," he replied. He was a heart surgeon from Tucson. We told him that Aharon was undergoing operations in Tucson and he made us promise that for our next operation, we would come to his home.

"Where are you headed?" I asked him.

He pointed at one of his two children and began to relate: "We named him 'Itai' after a fighter killed in the Second Lebanon War. 'Itai', the fighter was Itai Steinberger, a talented photographer and musician who had planned to study at the Betzalel Academy. He was killed when he was just twenty-one. He served in the crack unit, *Sayeret* 401, and he was shot to death while rescuing a wounded soldier during the Battle of Sulouqi. He left behind a letter to his parents in case he did not return. We have already said that every soldier who goes into battle knows he may not come home, or, that he may not return intact, and in the moment of battle, he decides to place his people's life before his personal life. For his heroism he received a citation. When the citation was announced, Itai's father said, "The citation that he received was for his love of his fellow man, his camaraderie, the encouragement he offered others, and for his leading the pack . . ."

"What is your connection to the fallen?" I asked the Tucson physician.

"There is no connection," he replied. "My wife and I heard his story, and it greatly impressed us. Now we are flying to Israel because a memorial ceremony is being held in Itai's memory. We decided to attend the ceremony and to meet the family, whom we do not know at all."

A Jew, who was born in the United States and lives there, had named his son after someone he did not know, and he named him "Itai" at that, not an American name. Could there be any greater expression of the exile drawing closer to the Jewish People and State on its day of celebration?

Part VI | New Beginnings

A Second Banquet of Thanksgiving

During the course of our preparations for the third operation, we had begun planning and organizing a public banquet of thanksgiving. The date earmarked was May 14, three weeks after the third operation. On the one hand, we wanted to include as many people as possible in this banquet. Many people were partners with us in our moments of trembling and prayer. Many people had never left us up to that very moment. Also due to our desire to publicize the miracle and our thanks we tended towards a larger banquet. On the other hand, how big should it be? Three hundred people? Five hundred? Was that not too much? Who would be insulted if he was not invited? Some people would come even if not invited. For example, the Army Chief-of-Staff had told us a half year before that he was coming whether we wanted it or not. We deliberated, moving forward with our decisions.

Aharon still had an indentation between his left ear and eye, one that it had been impossible to fill in during the operation in which they implanted replacement material in his skull. It had been impossible both due to a medical problem and due to a small oversight during the operation. For months already we had been exploring the possibility of filling in the area replacement material. We learned that the physicians in Israel and abroad had had no experience with this, yet all were willing to try. We decided, in conjunction with Rav Firer, to wait several months and only then to explore the possibilities.

Indeed, the banquet would not be held at the end of all the operations and treatments. You could say that most of that was behind us, but not all of it. And no one knew when and if all of it would be behind us. It was clear to us that we had experienced many miracles. We knew we had had the good fortune to have Aharon return to his old self. We knew there would be other such difficulties, but we were thankful for all that Aharon had.

A year and three months after the injury, the telephone rang. The caller was a member of the Beilinson Hospital medical staff, and he informed us that he had left his job at the hospital.

"Why?" we asked.

His oblique, hesitant response was, "No. You don't need to know." So I said, "If you called, that's a sign that it is important to us."

"I am in a sort of battle shock from the sight of Aharon and of Ben Schpitzer after the injury," he said, and then he added, "People with I.D.F. injuries look worse than people with any other kind of injuries. Dealing with the wounded, touching amputated stumps, is hard."

We remained silent. Scripture states, "You will be driven mad by what your eyes behold" (Deuteronomy 28:34). It's hard not to go mad and to have nightmares after seeing a deformed person. Maybe the biggest surprise is that not more people who come in contact with the severely wounded like Aharon suffer trauma and feel as though the earth has been pulled out from under their feet.

We chatted and set a time to meet. This was a wonderful person who had cared for Aharon devotedly, and had always tried to ease his suffering and to help him to improve. I prayed that the disruption he was suffering would strengthen him and invest him with new vigor.

We returned from the third operation, and banquet preparations went into high gear. Once more there were deliberations, and even a few arguments, about the number of people who should be invited and on the nature of the banquet. Once more we were struggling between the desire to shout out loud for all to

see, "Look at the great miracle and believe it is possible to perse-
vere, even when a sharp sword is pressed against one's throat," i.e.,
the desire to thank G-d publicly, versus the desire for quiet and
modesty, for intimacy, the small, still voice.

At one of the services in the Tucson synagogue, my glance
befell a large sign hanging on the wall, explaining "*Modim*", the
blessing of thanks from the Shemoneh Esreh, which includes the
words, "We thank You, O L-rd our G-d . . . for Your miracles that
are with us daily." In English, that blessing is called "Thanksgiving", i.e., *giving* thanks. You don't *say* thank you and you don't
take anything. Rather, you *give* thanks. Thanks is tied to giving.
Whoever feels like he deserves everything cannot give thanks.
You need the trait of giving in order truly to give thanks, and not
just to say thank you.

Amidst the calls I was making to announce the banquet, I received an email of the sort intended not just for you but for a large
audience. Someone was certain that "there are stories that have to
be publicized, and that this was one of them".

This story is truly astounding, even after so many surprises:

Dvir Emanueloff was the first soldier killed in the Gaza Cast
Lead war. His father had died two years previous, from a ma-
lignancy, and Dvir, as the only son amongst daughters, bore
the entire burden together with his mother, Dalia. Dvir's death
caused particularly great suffering, due to his being an only
son, thus leaving only the women of the house . . .

One day, one of his sisters asked their mother to come with
her to a Jerusalem fair, where there was supposed to be an
interesting performance. Their mother was not so interested.
She felt down in the dumps, yet she also did not wish to sadden
her daughter, so she agreed, and she went there with her without a lot of joy or interest.

The performance took place at Sultan's Pool. While the
musicians were warming up, and the performance was being
delayed a bit, a two-year-old toddler approached her, with
golden curls, looking like an angel, and touched her shoulder.
Dalia, who works as a pre-school teacher, turned her head,

saw the little angel face, and began a conversation with him.

– What's your name?

– Eshel.

– Would you like to be my friend, Eshel?

– Yes.

– Would you like to sit by me?

– Yes.

The parents, sitting two rows above, watched their angel "harassing" the older woman and they called him to them. Dalia, for her part, calmed them down and told them that everything was all right. Then little Eshel told her that he had a baby brother named Dvir . . . Dalia was taken aback by the name, and she climbed the two rows to Eshel's parents, saw the infant in the stroller and told them sort of apologetically, "If you don't mind my asking, how old is your son?" and they answered, "Half a year old". And then she added, "Once again, if you don't mind my prying, was he born before or after Cast Lead?" and they replied, "After". And then again, "I'm really sorry! This will be my last question: Why did you call him Dvir?" Shiri, Eshel and Dvir's mother, told the following story:

"I am an I.D.F. officer in charge of the wounded, and when I was at the end of my pregnancy with Dvir, the doctors feared that they had discovered a very serious birth defect in the infant. Yet since it was at the very end, it was impossible to do a thing, but to wait for the birth and to see if there really was a defect or not. So, I went home after the examination and at home I heard about the death of Dvir in battle, and I immediately made a 'deal' with G-d: If You let me have a healthy baby, I promise to call him Dvir after the soldier Dvir who was killed."

Dalia, mother of the soldier Dvir, said with mouth agape, "I am Dvir's mother."

The young parents did not believe her.

"Really, I am Dvir's mother," said Dalia, and still they did not believe her and they asked, "What is your name?"

"Dalia," said. "Dalia Emanuelov from Pisgat Zeev . . ."

Then the mother of little Dvir said to Dalia, "Take Dvir into your lap. Dvir wants to give you a hug."

One of our sons was preparing for the banquet a film summarizing everything we had been through. He told me that Tzvia had suggested including in the film the speech Aharon had made at his engagement party.

"Is there a tape of it?" I asked.

"Yes," he answered. Tzvia's sister had videotaped it."

I wanted to hear how Aharon had spoken before his injury. Aharon spoke about the obligation to give thanks and the joy of every person over what he has, and about the need to give thanks to the Creator even when facing hardships and suffering. I said to myself: Amazing! If we present the video without saying when it was from, everyone will think it was from *after* the injury.

Thirteen months after the injury, Aharon spoke more slowly, and occasionally got stuck on words when he talked, but besides that issue of speed, there was almost no recognizable difference between that video and his recent speech.

Thursday, precisely a year and four months after the injury, we held our banquet of thanksgiving to the Master of the Universe, and likewise to His emissaries, for saving Aharon and for his return to normal life, even if several problems still remained.

At 7:30 PM, guests were starting to arrive. People were coming on time, and that's not typical in our country. We announced an opening reception for 7:30 on the assumption that people would start to arrive at 8:00. Yet surprise! Not this time. Here were Aharon's brigade commander and battalion commander, Aharon's soldiers, family members, the physicians and medics who had taken care of Aharon, and other invitees. I had never been at such a large banquet of thanksgiving, and I did not know exactly what to expect. In the last few days, people had been calling and asking, "What is the evening's schedule? When will it be over?" and I answered, "I don't really know how the evening will advance and when we will finish." The entire evening I was more excited than I had ever been. My children told me afterwards that they didn't recall me ever speaking in so unorganized a fashion as I had at that banquet.

The crowd was rather eclectic. It included a couple who define themselves as atheists, a cousin of Chaya whom until that moment had never been over the Green Line, and had decided to see what a banquet of thanksgiving is, commanders and soldiers from all sectors of the population, and Hareidim who assist us with all our flights abroad.

Brigadier General Herzi HaLevi, Aharon's brigade commander in the war, spoke about diversity and the need for our sense of unity as a people. He also related that some time ago he had come to Aharon and Tzvia's house "to talk about Aharon's having been called up right after his wedding." He did not elaborate.

We showed the film about the period we had been through from the wedding until now. The atmosphere was electrified. You could have collected many cups of tears during the twelve minutes of the film. Aharon spoke and afterwards I summed up the special period we had been through and were still going through. The assembled rose to dance. The evening ended at 11:00 PM.

One of Aharon's yeshiva teachers told me at the end of the evening, "I had another affair I was supposed to be at, but I could not leave this one." The atheist couple told me, "The terminology we heard this evening was very different from our own, but we believe the intent was not far off." That is, they call themselves atheists, but I call them saints. As I have said and said again, not everything seen and heard on surface is what lies beneath the surface.

We decided that this banquet would be closed to the media, and, indeed, no one from the media heard about it. The next morning, the phone started ringing. "We heard that there was a banquet with a photographer. Could we have copies of the pictures and videos? We'd be willing to pay the photographer!

The Birth

One morning, towards the end of Tzvia's eighth month of pregnancy, I answered my cell phone. It was Aharon. "Dad, we spent all night in the hospital, and now we're coming home."

"What happened?' I asked. "What fun, Dad! We were in the hospital and not because of me! The reason is even something good. Tzvia had premature contractions, but everything is all right and we are on our way home."

Suddenly I understood Aharon's feelings every time we went to the hospital for a check-up or for surgery. It's a feeling that's not simple or easy to deal with. And now he was in the hospital not because of his injury. What is the greater miracle? The birth of a new infant or Aharon's rebirth after being mortally wounded?

We were invited to a Disabled Veterans' evening honoring Rabbi Ronsky in Ra'anana. It was amazing to see the great love of so many of those veterans for Rav Ronsky. We heard about his great devotion to those veterans. He encourages them and comes to help out at all hours of the day and night, and always with a smile.

On the way home, Aharon shared with me the tribulations of his friend, who suffers from poor relations with his wife. "How fortunate I am that I am not in his situation." Better to be wounded than to live in a morose state such as his."

His words were expressed naturally, and Aharon did not understand, presumably until reading these words, just how much they touched my heart and what happened inside me when I heard them. Great stores of good health reverberated with every letter and word uttered by Aharon, a health that very few healthy people are privileged to have.

Wednesday Morning I received a call from a close friend, Colonel (res.) Geva, who established an organization that brings to the public at large – in schools, kibbutzim and the army – values that are the *aqua vita* of man's spirit and of the Jewish People. In these times, when people are chiefly preoccupied with the physical and the superficial, they are starting to feel a thirst for such living waters.

He said to me: "Tonight I am flying to the United States for important meetings. Come there with me." To this day I do not understand what made me answer yes. A flight to the U.S. unconnected with surgery for Aharon seemed bizarre to me.

In the course of a single, very intensive week, we met with the Jewish community of New York, religious and irreligious, Zionists and Hareidim, the very wealthy and the dirt poor. Many felt as though the hour glass of the Jews in the U.S. is running out. A White House reporter pronouncing that the Jews of Israel have to return to Poland and to Germany, and other bizarre occurrences, did not bode well for the Jews. As is well known, there has not been one Jewish community during the past two thousand years of exile, that has not undergone pogroms and ultimately been forced to leave.

The media reported what had happened with the "Peace Flotilla" transporting a gang of Al-Qaeda terrorists. The moment the results of Israel's commandeering the flotilla became known, a global lynch burst forth like a demon held in a bottle for many years. In the NRG website there was a video clip of an anti-Israel demonstration held in Los Angeles. Dozens of Arabs demonstrated, denigrating Israel. Amongst all the demonstrators there suddenly appeared a young boy with a yarmulke and a gigantic Israeli flag, walking amongst the demonstrators. Tempers flared. There were shouts to kill the boy. Yet he, as though he could not hear, continued walking amongst the demonstrators with a calm, tranquil countenance. Police asked him to leave the site but he continued, About seven policemen protected him, walking wherever he walked. That man, going against the current, taught us more than anything about our status as a nation running against the current. If we have faith in our path, then we can survive and swim, even against the current. If, however, we lose our erect bearing, then the current will sweep us away.

We met with the owner of a non-kosher restaurant chain in New York, whose son serves in the Golani Brigade and want to be an Israeli combat soldier. He was caught coming to the base with a car and was punished with military jail time.

"My son wants so much to be a combat soldier. Why did they knock the wind out of his sails?" his father asked.

"Why did he enlist?" I asked. "Because he is crazy," answered the father.

There are a lot of crazies in the Jewish People.

I received a call from Miami. A friend told of a woman named Ruth who owns oil fields. She heard our story and she wanted to meet us. We decided that Geva would fly down to Florida and I would stay in New York for an interview on New York Jewish Radio.

Geva returned and reported on a unique, bizarre meeting. Ruth is seventy-five, full of vigor and young blood. She is certain she is Jewish but has no proof. She is ready to undergo Orthodox conversion and she is asking for help. She explained that in her view, Obama is an anti-Semite and many Jews will move to Israel during the coming decade. She, too, wants to move and to help out with the future wave of Aliya. "Well," I thought to myself, ours is a bizarre, complex world."

I returned from the United States.

Tuesday, the Creation day G-d twice called "good", the 26th of the Hebrew month of Sivan, 5770, at 1:00 PM, Aharon called and said, "Mazel tov! We had a baby girl!" I was filled with joy. My eyes brimmed with tears, looking for a way to burst forth. I recalled the reaction of the director of the Rehabilitation Department on hearing the news that Tzvia was pregnant: "It's a miracle." She repeated it several times. Aharon's critical head injury was liable to cause many bizarre types of damage, including inhibiting the ability to bring new life into the world. A year and five months after they thought Aharon would not remain among the living, he was privileged not just to be alive but to bring new life into the world.

Every birth is a miracle. How is it that out of nothing, or in the Mishna's words, out of "a putrid drop", a creature with such a complex, miraculous structure emerges? It has blood vessels, sinews, muscles, nerves, the ability to think, emotions, to the point that everybody is able to carry on harmonious, peaceful relations with one another. Yet birth, itself, is a miracle, within a miracle, within a miracle.

An hour-and-a-half after the birth, the flood of calls from the media began full force. No newspaper in Israel, Hebrew or English, and no television channel or radio station failed to call and ask for an interview regarding the birth.

People say that "dog bites man" is not news, but "man bites dog" is news. Generally the media looks for and accentuates problems. Suddenly, they were pining to announce a birth to the public. They realized the story of the birth would be a "good sell" with the public. Why?

I surfed the Internet news stations. Ynet and NRG both told about the miracle birth and the hero who became a father. I read the talkbacks. Many wrote that finally they were reading about something good happening in the news. Weren't they looking for "action"? From the Internet I learned about names that purportedly had already been given to our new granddaughter, such as "Nesli" [a miracle to me], "Nurit" [light], and various, bizarre alternatives.

Wednesday Morning, all the newspapers devoted half a page or more to the birth. "Victory Birth" exulted one headline. Another cried out, "Daddy!" "Double Miracle Birth" cried a third. All the radio and television stations quoted things Aharon had said in the past. On Friday, Aharon and Tzvia were photographed with the new baby for the "*Yediot Aharonot*" daily newspaper, with the headline, "Cast Lead Hero Presents New Daughter: 'We were privileged to bring forth new life.'" The Prime Minister, the Chief-of-Staff, generals and government ministers called and offered their best wishes. Hearing their voices, one could tell that their joy was sincere.

The wave of phone calls increased the moment Shabbat was over. Over the receiver I heard, "This is the CEO of a toy company. We'd like to have your address so we can send toys for Aharon and Tzvia in honor of the new infant's birth." They sent toys. Boy did they send toys! Two days after the call, I received a box a meter-and-a-half by a meter square containing expensive toys. "We wanted to say Mazel tov. This infant is the daughter of the entire Jewish People," said another spokesman.

A dental clinic in Kfar Saba sent its blessings, etc., etc. Gifts came in from all over Israel and letters came in from the Diaspora, demonstrating once more that many people felt this was the daughter of every single Jew.

It seems as though the flood of calls from the media and from the Jewish People was even greater than after the injury. Once more I had trouble understanding. One of the teachers in my yeshiva high school, Dorit, newly religious, told me that her father, who is not religious, had called her last week and had said, "You know what? Today is a very happy day. A baby girl was born to Aharon Karov." Dorit immediately added, "He does not know that I know you." He told me without knowing it."

My wife told me that as part of her work, she met with a bereaved mother who told her, "Aharon's injury left some kind of scar on the hearts of the entire Jewish People. Now that a girl has been born to him, it's a sort of recovery for everyone."

Two calls particularly moved me. One was from the mother of a soldier killed in Cast Lead, who said, "We would like to wish you a mazel tov. It really makes us happy." I swallowed hard. I still found it difficult to respond and to utter a word in such conversations. What fortitude is required of a mother who lost her son to call a father whose son was spared and is now celebrating joyous occasions like the birth of a daughter? It would seem that enormous strengths are hidden away in the human spirit. Only special experiences cause those strengths to flow from the depths of the spirit to mundane life.

The second call was from the sister of Benny, of blessed memory. As you may recall, Benny was killed in a car accident three days after Aharon was injured. We met the family in Intensive Care and since then we have been very close. "Mazel tov!" she said. "We were very happy to hear about the birth of your granddaughter."

The Ashkenazic custom is that when a girl is born, the father is called up to the Torah to name her publicly. Until that official naming, it is customary not to reveal the name. It can happen that parents decide on a name and then, at the last moment, decide to change it.

Minutes before Shabbat, Aharon called me to inform me of their daughter's name. A person's name is not just a way to address him. It also says something about his essence. G-d orchestrates the thoughts in the parents' minds and hearts and this leads to their giving the name.

There are people in my family who tense up before an infant is named, but not I. I feel like I know what the name will be. I told the family that there could only be one appropriate name, and that is "Hodaya", Hebrew for "thanksgiving". There is a fierce, profound desire to give thanks, to thank the Master of the Universe, to give thanks to His emissaries and to thank the entire Jewish People.

"Your granddaughter will be named 'Hodaya'. Mazel tov," said Aharon. We wished each other "Shabbat Shalom" and concluded the conversation.

Seeing up to the Heart

One of my sons brought me the book, "*U'kratem Dror*" [Proclaim Liberty], which tells about the late Colonel Dror Weinberg. Dror, a highly respected officer, was the Hebron Brigade Commander when he was killed in a battle with terrorists. The book is a collection of short stories about Dror, told by people who met him during his life. I was especially taken with the story of Robert, a news photographer, regarding his encounter with Dror at a Paratroopers' Brigade event at Beit She'an.

> I was particularly impressed by the natural way Dror behaved with other officers, on the one hand, while blending in easily with the soldiers of the battalion on the other. I took many pictures of him, shaking hands with the Commander-in-Chief, slapping the back of the head of the Central Command, hugging the first sergeant, and offering a "Job well done!" to the combat support company. I told him so at the end of the ceremony. "Do you know what my secret is?" he asked, immediately answering his own question: "My height". I must admit I had a hard time understanding what he meant.
>
> "Do you know who Reb Arye Levin was?" he then asked. "The saint of Jerusalem. Never heard of him?!" he asked, surprised, as though I know saints personally.

Dror told me about Reb Arye Levin. When he heard that somebody was avoiding a meeting with him because that person went bareheaded and embarrassed in his presence, Reb Arye said, "Don't worry. I am short. I don't see if you've got a kippa on your head. I only see up to the heart." Dror went on, "I, too, am short. I don't see the rank insignias on people's shoulders. I just see up to the heart. If someone gives his heart, I am with him."

What a story! I thought to myself: We look at the surface too much. The ranks on the shoulders, the car, the hair color and the whole outer appearance.

The media dealt at length with the High Court ruling ordering that parents from Emanuel who refused to send their children to the local school for "educational" reasons be imprisoned. Tensions rose. Hareidim against secular, the court against the rabbis. I know that beneath all the shouting and wars, there is more that unites than that divides. Has not the time come to educate ourselves to deepen our perspective, to stop seeing the shoulder insignias, the outer dress, and to learn to see the heart?

Two thousand years of exile. Such a long time did not succeed in blotting out the emotion that makes Jews care for one another. Yet it did succeed in concealing it. We give it free rein only in special times like wars, and around stories like that of Aharon. Our sages said, "What G-d wants is the heart." The heart is hidden away and is not revealed for all to see, but only for those who ponder life deeply.

Closing the Circle

Tuesday, July 13, precisely a year-and-a-half after the injury, Aharon made an appointment with Dr. Jackson, in which the latter would show him pictures from the original operation. It was important to Aharon to know in what condition he arrived in the hospital.

"Why is it important for you to see how you looked then?" I asked. "You know you didn't look so great . . ."

Aharon answered that he knew, but he still wanted to see.

I drove to a meeting with the Head of the Central Command. Along the way, two news correspondents called me. One was from Channel 2 and the other was from a popular newspaper. The newspaper was already thinking about Rosh Hashana. They wanted to write a long, optimistic feature article containing our story, and Channel 2 was thinking about an end-of-the-year T.V. special.

A year-and-a-half had gone by. It had been an eighteen-month trek into the personal life of Aharon, and from my point of view, also eighteen months of concrete discovery that the Jewish People live on, and that the spirit of our father Abraham still beats in Israel's heart, even if below the surface.

At the end of the meeting with the Head of the Central Command, I called to ask Aharon how his meeting had gone with Dr. Jackson. "It was hard but it did me good," Aharon answered. It was hard for me to understand the need for this, and hard to understand the good that Aharon felt.

A week later, Tuesday, was the Ninth of Av, 5770, a day earmarked for soul searching over the Temple's destruction. It is a day on which it is important for the entire nation to stop, take a break, ponder the future, and consider how they can let the good, unifying sides of life take ascendancy and be revealed in all their might.

Tisha Be'Av, as I have said, is also Aharon's birthday. Each year we delay the celebration in favor of the national soul searching. All the years we marked his birthday a day or two after the fast day. This year, however, we could not push off a birthday that was not to be taken for granted. We were not far from marking this day without Aharon, G-d forbid. We were very fortunate.

Aharon, Tzvia and Hodaya arrived on Tisha Be'Av afternoon to complete the fast day with us and celebrate Aharon's birthday after the fast. Aharon told me a bit about the pictures he had seen from the operation. A year-and-a-half after the fact I made a discovery of no small import. "I saw that seven metal shards entered my brain. Six were removed in the operation and the seventh, which penetrated deeper, is still there," Aharon said. We were certainly aware of the large piece of shrapnel that had allowed itself to take a stroll in Aharon's brain and had remained there. Yet we had not known about the six that were removed, and perhaps we did not wish to know. I recall the doctors saying, "We cleaned out all we could without doing too much damage to the brain." Now it turned out that this "cleaning out" process included removing six shards. If I needed any more proof of how much I do not know and do not fathom the miracle, I received it once again.

Aharon told me that he saw a picture of his left ear full of blood and shrapnel. I recall that that first night, after it became known that Aharon had been wounded from a powerful mine that had blown up over his head, I asked the director of Intensive Care, Professor Singer, whether there had been any damage to his ears. Had his eardrums remained intact and not been damaged? Professor Singer told me that he did not know. He said that he had checked and seen that there was no visible damage. Today we know that the insignificant damage to Aharon's left ear is a very light sign of what his ears underwent in the explosion.

I called Ofer Schpitzer, Ben's father. We occasionally exchange notes on what is happening with each other's sons. From Ofer's cell phone burst forth the voice of Yehoram Gaon singing, "Hello there, wonderful land! Your humble servant sings a song of praise." No small number of cynics would respond to that song, "It's not so wonderful and he's no servant."

As I have already said, the question is how we relate to the reality. One can emphasize the problems or one can emphasize the positive. What I see and how I assess it depend on my worldview.

I add my voice to that of Yehoram Gaon: "Hello there, wonderful land! Your humble service sings a song of praise." Yet simultaneously I raise up a prayer for the problems to be rectified, and I strive with all my meager strength to advance and to repair things in our little land.

Everyone's Story

Two weeks after Hodaya's birth I went to the Western Wall to recite my afternoon prayers. I had a hard time reaching those vast, unique stones. With every step I was forced to stop. "Mazel tov! Very happy for you!" said someone whose head covering was apparently not a permanent fixture.

Suddenly I met a rabbi who was a bereaved father. His son was a drill sergeant in the elite "Egoz" unit, and he was killed in an accident during maneuvers. We meet every once in a while at conventions. Generally, we shake hands in greeting, as is the normal custom. This time I was privileged to receive a strong, brave hug and a kiss. "Mazel tov!" We were so happy to hear about the birth of your granddaughter." I was overwrought.

Even amidst my prayers people approached me and shook my hand. On a day of troublesome news – the Turkish flotilla; the Emanuel-High Court confrontation, and more, people remembered and shared in the joy of Aharon and his family. I was surprised. I was also surprised by my still being surprised. Why had we merited this love? Am I worthy of it? Certainly not! Yet perhaps there are things that can be truly seen only beneath the surface? Aharon said to me, "I knew that during war time people unite together and show concern for one another, but via joy? How could so many people be joyous over the birth of our daughter?

Three weeks after Hodaya's birth, letters were still arriving. "To Aharon Karov – Ariel". They did not know the precise address. They were optimists. They hoped the letter would reach its destination and, indeed, it did. Many letters came to our own address as well.

I called the dental clinic to set up an appointment, as I did once every two years. There was a new secretary. "This is Zeev Karov speaking," I said.

"Zeev Tabor?" she asked. "No, Karov," I responded, stressing my words.

"Is this your first time?"

"No," I answered.

"Please wait."

"Look Aharon Karov. The following date is . . ."

I stopped and reminded her, "This is *Zeev* Karov." There was confusion on the other end of the line.

"Sorry. You know, there's that wounded officer. I pray for him a lot."

Just one more time I was unsure whether to reveal I am his father, or to leave it at that.

Was the issue here a miracle from heaven? Was it just Aharon's fortitude and our own, that of Aharon's family? Perhaps the issue was Aharon's fortitude and the fortitude of the entire Jewish People? And perhaps all these factors together?

A year and eight months after the injury, we were coming home from another operation in the United States. It was a Tuesday, and my wife and I were celebrating our thirtieth wedding anniversary.

I entered a gift shop at the Sirkin Junction Mall in Petach Tikva. The saleslady was a woman about thirty-five years old. She was wearing a tee shirt and had a tattoo on her arm. I perused the store's shelves and tried to find an appropriate gift.

"You've bought her before, haven't you?"

"No," I answered.

"Are you sure? You look very familiar to me," she said.

"No, I've never been here," I repeated with certainty, continuing to examine the shelves.

Yet she would not give up. After a few minutes she asked, "So why do you look so familiar to me?"

I gave up. "Apparently you've seen me in the media," I said.

"Why?" she continued.

"Because my son was wounded in the war . . ."

She began to tremble and to weep.

"That's it! You're those optimistic heroes! I would like to send a gift to Aharon and his wife." She immediately left the cash register and looked for something she considered appropriate. She spotted one item and put it in a bag. She spotted something else and added it. "Remind me of his wife's name, please?"

"Tzvia," I said.

"Right!"

She then sat down by the cash register and wrote a letter of greeting to Aharon and to Tzvia.

On our home answering machine, a message was waiting from

Gross, a kibbutznic from the North: "I was so happy to hear about the birth of a daughter to Aharon. When I heard, I said to myself, 'The Jewish People live on!'"

Was I surprised or not? I don't know.

I was reminded of the thank you note that my older daughter and her husband sent to the guests who came to gladden them on their wedding day. In the letter they quoted from the philosopher Asher Ginsberg, better known as *"Ahad HaAm"*:

> *A strong nationalist passion must beat deep in everyone's heart, until no Jew can find contentment solely based on his own personal happiness. We must all raise the name of Jerusalem above our chiefest joy. Then faith will derive automatically, and deeds will follow.*

It seems as though Aharon's story captured the hearts of many of our people because it actually involves the deepest, most hidden longings within the heart of each and every one of us. It is everybody's story.

Final Word

There is no final word, no end of the story. Both our personal story and the national story carry on, and will continue to develop. Aharon is almost entirely back to his old self. He testifies about himself that following the injury he has become a happier person. He delivers lectures to youth. There is one more operation before us, and he is still undergoing treatment in the outpatient Rehabilitation clinic of Tel HaShomer.

The Jewish People, for their part, must strive to uncover the marvelous treasures hidden within them. At a time when those treasures are awakening and coming to light, there is no end to this process.

Epilogue

I sent my writings to an editor. I was uncertain whether to publish them or to leave them hidden with me, and a decision was called for. A man I very much admire, a very experienced writer, prodded me to move forward. After hearing stories from me about our encounters, he "forced" me to write, and since then I have been putting everything in writing.

I was uncertain regarding what to write about and what not to write about. What should be revealed and what should remain concealed? Not everything had to be exposed. Regarding some things, discretion was better for both them and for the world. Others were best off being shared. I chiefly recorded things tied to our encounter with the Jewish People in Israel and the Diaspora.

A week went by after I sent off the materials, and I received the following response:

"On simple reflection this book is impossible. It cannot be that this is the reality. Everything sounds kitchy, too perfect, too strong, too powerful, too implausible. The optimism and fortitude you broadcast are so powerful . . . sometimes the even the handwriting generates negative feelings – perhaps even anger at the naivety, the suppression. Yet all the negative feelings and the harsh, unclear thoughts are simply swept away with the tears . . .

"So the story is still coming into being, and closing the circle on this exciting, amazing story will symbolize not just the birth of a book . . . a book that will become an important document in the Israeli consciousness, strengthening, exalting and enriching us with hope."

I pondered these words and sentences and my heart pounded. On the one hand, I knew that my writing contained not even the slightest exaggeration. As far as I was concerned, I had offered a dry account of what we had been through. The days, the stories, the names, the events – all of them, without exception, were the absolute truth.

On the other hand, the emphasis had been on the half of the cup that was full. I did not relate all the problems we had experienced and the mishaps we had suffered. The writing contained only part of the story. Even the good and marvelous things that I wrote were very little of what we experienced. Yet, from my point of view, they represented the main part, the essence of the reality and the essence of our feelings.

"Naivety"? Am I naïve? I am reminded of the physician who explained to my son-in-law, Assaf, that he must "bring Aharon's father down to reality". This was after on the first day of the injury I expressed my faith and prayer that Aharon would succeed in returning to us, and I told the family that we had a long road ahead of us. At the time, the doctors were certain that Aharon had only a few hours to live.

I ran to my *Even-Shoshan* Dictionary to see the precise definition of the word "naïve". I found two entries: (1) lacking wisdom, and (2) simple, unsophisticated, direct.

I truly think that the story is simple and direct. It is very unsophisticated. I am not used to such writing. I am used to the wise, profound writing of what is called "the *Mussar* literature", the Jewish ethical tracts. I pondered to myself: there are times when precisely the simple things are the most profound and surprising. We have become a very sophisticated, philosophical society, for whom it is hard to see the simple truth. It seems as though the simple truth confuses us.

"Implausible" . . . "Too powerful". I really do not feel powerful. We found ourselves in an extremely harrowing situation. It involved a change in our way of life. We faced enormous fears and worries, but there was also a great deal of hope, faith and success.

"Too perfect"? Our story is not perfect. Our path was strewn with ups and downs, and it still goes on. I also know that there are a lot of stories that end sadly. Yes, I remember Benny, the reservist. I remember the other wounded who are today in worse condition that Aharon. Not a day goes by that I do not mention their names in prayer. I beg of G-d: Send them a speedy and a complete recovery!

After Aharon's promotion to Lieutenant

Aharon and Tzvia on their wedding night

During Operation Cast Lead, two days after his wedding and before his injury

Aharon's father, Rav Karov, with Boogi Ya'Alon about a week after the injury

Rabbi Karov with General Gabi Ashkenazi

Prime Minister Benjamin Netanyahu visiting Aharon a week after his injury at Belinson hospital

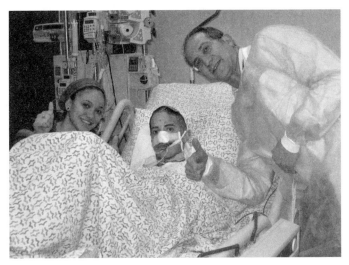

With wife Tzvia and Dr. Jackson shortly after one of the head surgeries

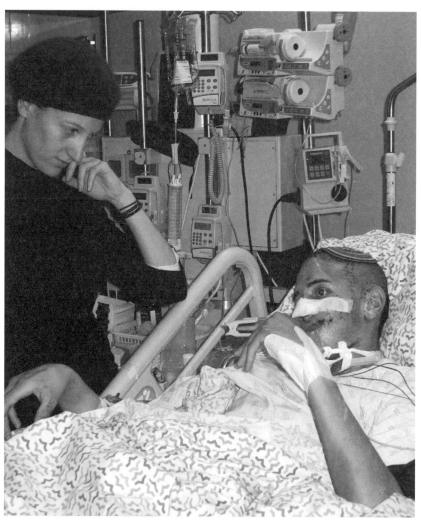

3 weeks after his injury, with older sister Miriam at Belinson hospital

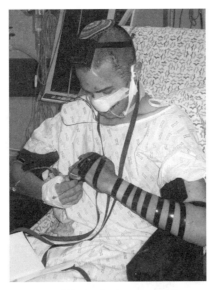

Putting on Tefillin for the first time after his injury

Reporters at Aharon's first public appearance 3 weeks after his injury

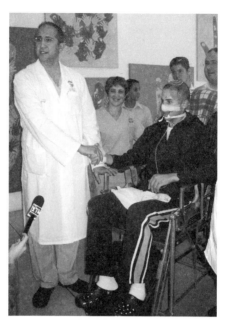

Receiving Dr. Jackson's famous approval before his first transfer to a different hospital

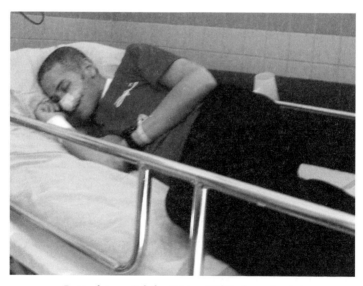

Resting between Rehab activities at Tel Hashomer hospital

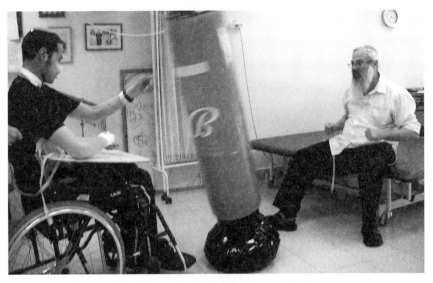

Aharon and his father at the rehab facility three months after the injury

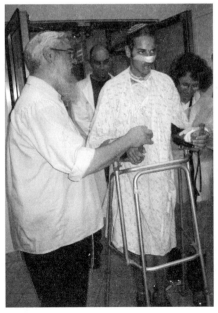

Aharon's first few steps at the Tel Hashomer rehab facility

Home with his mother Chaya, four months after his injury

The first time Aharon came home, 4 months after his injury, with his wife Tzvia

With My Israel volunteers after the birth of Aharon's son, Amitzur.

With Dr. Jackson at a Seudat Hodaya, 18 months after the injury

With singer Avraham Fried at a concert, two years after the injury

Speaking to a group of high school students in Lod.

IDF Chief Rabbi Rafi Peretz with Aharon, his father and Panim el Panim founder Colonel (res.) Geva Rapp

During Operation Pillar of Defense, speaking to visitors from the US

*Running the NYC marathon,
November 2013*

*At the marathon finish line,
receiving a medal.*

*Passing the marathon medal to the parents of Major (z"l) Benaya Rein, who was
killed while rescuing wounded soldiers under heavy fire in the Second Lebanon War.
Major (z"l) Rein, was Aharon's neighbor at Karnei Shomron.*